AMAZING AND EXTRAORDINARY FACTS

UNDERGROUND
RAILWAYS OF THE WORLD

UNDERGROUND
RAILWAYS OF THE WORLD

Stephen Halliday

RYDON
PUBLISHING

A Rydon Publishing Book
35 The Quadrant
Hassocks
West Sussex
BN6 8BP
www.rydonpublishing.co.uk
www.rydonpublishing.com

First published by Rydon Publishing in
2021

A CIP catalogue record for this book is
available from the British Library.

ISBN: 978-1-910821-40-4

THE AUTHOR

Stephen Halliday is a British
historian specializing in transport,
military, architecture and
industrial history.
He is the author of a number
of titles in our *Amazing &
Extraordinary Facts* series, including
*Great Britain, Cathedrals and
Abbeys, London Underground* and
London at War.
He contributes articles and
reviews to magazines such as
*Literary Review, Times Higher
Education, BBC History* and
History Today.

PICTURE CREDITS

CONTENTS

INTRODUCTION

In January 1863 London's Metropolitan Railway, running from Paddington to Farringdon, in the heart of the City of London, became the world's first underground railway. It was a success from its earliest days but others were slow to follow. By 1900 London had been joined by only three others in this novel means of transporting large numbers of people in cities without over-burdening their congested streets. Budapest and Glasgow followed London in 1896 with their own smaller systems and in 1900 Paris added its 'Métro', built in time for the Paris Exhibition which marked the opening of the new century. It took its name from London's Metropolitan Railway. By the outbreak of World War II in 1939 another ten cities had joined the underground club, with one in South America (Buenos Aires): two in the USA (New York and Philadelphia); two in Japan (Tokyo and Osaka); and five in Europe (Berlin, Hamburg, Athens, Barcelona and Madrid). Many of the early systems were only a few kilometres in length with some tracks above ground. After World War II, Metros gathered pace and by the start of the 21st century 100 were in use with every continent having several except Australia which had to wait until 2019 before Sydney's entered service. But the 21st century has been the best time to be an underground railway engineer. Since the first year of the century, 79 underground railways have entered service and 31 are under construction or planned, most of these in Asia, with Chinese cities leading the way. Beijing has the greatest length of track, with 698 km (433.7 miles), though Shanghai, with 676 km (420 miles), is catching up and the two Chinese giants are also vying for the title of most used, with both approaching 4 billion passengers a year. By contrast Rennes, in France, has 9 km (5.5 miles) of track and carries 35 million passengers. The deepest station in Europe is that of Admiralteyskaya, in St Petersburg, at 86 metres

(282 feet) below ground and was built in the 1950s when such structures were created with a view to providing nuclear shelters. Hongtudi in the city of Chongqing in south-west China, is believed to have the world's deepest station, at 94 metres (308.4 feet), the passengers choosing between using escalators, which take 3 minutes 15 seconds to reach the platforms, or 354 steps. Details of construction are difficult to ascertain for some railways but the metro of North Korea's capital Pyongyang is believed to have lines 110 metres (360.8 feet) below the surface in which case it would have the deepest stations of all.

So at the time of writing, over 200 underground railways are in service or under construction. Many of great importance to their cities and passengers are otherwise unremarkable but others are of interest because of their history, the circumstances of their construction, the technical challenges they faced or the colourful personalities involved in their stories. This short volume aims to capture some of their amazing and extraordinary features.

Stephen Halliday
March 2021

Auckland: The City Rail Link

Auckland, the most populous city of New Zealand, with 1.7 million residents (the capital is the much smaller Wellington with 212,000) is at last to get an Underground Railway which will link two of its main line stations. Construction began in 2016 and is scheduled to be completed by 2024 at a projected cost of $4.4 billion (about £2.3 billion) though ominous hints of cost increases which are familiar to those associated with such projects have already been heard! The railway will be built to the narrow gauge 1067 mm (3 ft 6 in) which New Zealand shares with three Australian states (Queensland, Tasmania and Western Australia) and with a number of Far Eastern countries including Japan. It will be known as the *City Rail Link* and, besides connecting two main line stations, will have two new stations of its own. It will be 3.5 km (2.1 miles) in length and will use specially designed New Zealand Class AM electric multiple units built in Spain and drawing 25kv from overhead lines.

THE FRUIT OF SUCCESS
The Morningside Tunnel

New Zealand has 589 km (365.9 miles) of electrified passenger rail track though there is an additional 2,328 km (1,446.5 miles) of track for freight trains only. In July 2003 the Auckland City Council opened a new transport hub called the Britomart Centre with an underground terminal railway station and connecting bus services. It is to the north of the central business district of the city. The purpose of the venture was to encourage the use of public transport rather than private cars and such was the success of the venture that it was proposed that an underground rail link be built to connect the Britomart terminus with Auckland's other mainline station at Mount Eden across the central business area to the South.

As early as the 1920s it was proposed that a tunnel be built beneath the central area of Auckland called the Morningside tunnel. The idea was revived in various forms on several occasions during the 20th century, and was as often shelved on grounds of cost or practicality. The success of the Britomart transport hub breathed new life into the proposal, linked with the idea to build two new stations in the tunnel named Aotea and Karangahape, taking their names from the streets and squares above. These stations will give quicker access to the central business district and an upgrade to Mount Eden station will facilitate the passage of main line trains across the city between the two main terminals. In 2016 the New Zealand government announced that it would make funding available for the project, which was the signal for the work to begin.

DID YOU KNOW?

The works in the vicinity of Mount Eden will be built by Cut and Cover methods but the line will pass in double track tunnels beneath the central district for which a Tunnel Boring Machine has been designed and named after a determined woman, Dame Whina Cooper (1895–1994). Cooper was a teacher who campaigned for Maori land rights and specifically for the welfare of Maori women.

QUICK FACTS

THE FUTURE So Auckland now waits for its first underground railway while no doubt hoping that the costs do not follow the pattern set by Crossrail. And proposals are already being mooted for an extension of the system, with the first candidate a rail link to Auckland airport, New Zealand's principal air connection with the world.

Auckland skyline

Australia

There is change on the horizon for Australia as Sydney and Melbourne expand or adopt underground railway systems for their great cities.

MELBOURNE
City loop

M elbourne, with its population approaching 5 million, now vies with Sydney for the title of the most populous city in Australia. Founded in 1835 on the Yarra River, it takes its name from Lord Melbourne who was to become Queen Victoria's first Prime Minister. The city has long been provided with a good suburban rail network of surface trains, but it had to wait until the 1960s before the first plans were mooted for an underground system beneath the Central Business District to connect main line stations at Flinders Street and Spencer Street (later renamed Southern Cross). Progress in building the 12 km (7.4 miles) of what came to be known as the 'City Loop' was slow and construction, which began in 1971, was opened between 1981 and 1985 with five stations, of which three are underground – Flagstaff, Melbourne Central and Parliament.

In 2018 work started on an expansion of the system in the form of the 'Metro Tunnel' which will consist of two 9 km (5.5 mile) tunnels linking South Kensington station in the North West of the City with South Yarra station in the south–east. They are being built to the Australian broad gauge of 1600 mm (5 ft 3 in) and will draw electricity from overhead catenaries at 1500 volts DC. It is anticipated that the line will be completed by 2026.

SYDNEY METRO
The forgotten Home Secretary

Sydney, with its population just short of 5 million, is the oldest city in Australia and was founded in January 1788. The city took its name from the otherwise forgotten Lord Sydney, who was the British Home Secretary at the time. The city, with its huge harbour capable of accommodating, in the words of Governor Philip, 'a thousand sail of the line in the most perfect security', developed rapidly to become the largest city in Australia which at one time accommodated one fifth of the nation's entire population.

Plans for an underground railway were first mooted in 1915 by a railway engineer called John Bradfield who had visited New York and examined its Subway. The system, which opened in 1926, was in effect an extension of the existing suburban lines and linked Central station and Wynyard station with new underground stations at Town Hall, Circular Quay, St James and Museum. These are all heritage listed structures and in World War II some disused tunnels at St James were adapted for use as air raid shelters (fortunately never needed) and were later used for growing mushrooms. The trains were double deckers,

John Bradfield

drawing power from an overhead catenary at 1500 volts DC. After emerging from underground at Wynyard station the trains pass across Sydney Harbour on its celebrated bridge.

In 2001 the government announced a substantial extension of the network, beginning with a North–West Rail Link which opened in May 2019 linking Tallawong in the north west of the city to Chatswood on the northern outskirts, partly in tunnels and partly in cuttings. It consists of 36 km (22.3 miles) of standard gauge track serving 13 stations. Further extensions over the next five years will comprise approximately 77 additional km of track (47.8 miles) and a further 32 stations. 15.5 km (9.6 miles) of tunnel have already been bored by five tunnel boring machines with a view to linking the central business districts with the outer suburbs, the Olympic Park and Western Sydney Airport.

ROLLING STOCK AND SIGNALLING
INDIAN SINGLE DECKERS

The rolling stock for the new lines is being supplied by Alstom from its Indian factory and is, unusually for Sydney, of single deck design. It is equipped with communications based train control (CBTC) systems which use telecommunications to establish contacts between train, track and central control. This enables the precise location of the train to be identified and its movement and speed regulated accordingly, monitored by a central control unit. The system lends itself to automatic train operation, without the need for any staff on the train, including operating doors and detecting obstacles on the line.

Beijing Subway

FIRST IN MAINLAND ASIA

The Beijing Subway was the first to be built in China and in mainland Asia. It now consists of 16 lines, with 405 stations covering 690 km (428.7 miles) of track and carrying 3.9 billion passengers each year along with ten further suburban lines serving outer suburbs and airports. Fares are based on the distance travelled using cards which may be topped up like the Oyster cards used in London, 100 km (62.1 miles) of travel costing about 10 yuan, about £1. Senior citizens, army veterans and armed police travel free of charge. The tracks are laid to the standard gauge of 1435 mm (4 ft 8.5 in) with most of the trains running on 750 volts DC drawn from a third rail. Lines 14 and 16 run on 1500 volts DC drawn from an overhead catenary. Plans for monorails where the terrain is difficult for subterranean works have been discussed and reached advanced planning stages but have for the moment been shelved.

TROUBLE BETWEEN FRIENDS
The Great Leap Backwards

Beijing (formerly known as Peking) first became the capital of China in 1279 and resumed that position in 1949 (after two intervals when Nanking served as China's capital city) following the creation by Mao Tse-tung of the People's Republic of China with Beijing as its capital. Plans

for a subway for the capital were first mooted in 1953, with
early plans being drawn up by Soviet engineers who had
been involved in the construction of the Moscow Metro.
The plans were for a system of deep tunnels which, like those
of Moscow, would act as air raid shelters and be used for
moving troops as well as civilian passengers. The water table
in Beijing rendered this impractical and much of the system
was eventually built by 'Cut and Cover' methods, close to the
surface. Between 1953 and 1960, during a period of friendly
relations between the two Communist states, thousands of
Chinese students were sent to Moscow to study but this
ceased when ideological differences between the hard line
Communist party of China and the moderately liberalizing
agenda of Nikita Khrushchev's Russia led to a breakdown in
relations which became known in the West as the *Sino-Soviet
Split*. Plans for the Beijing subway were shelved. Further delays
were caused by Mao's 'Great Leap Forward' economic plan
which, between 1958 and 1962 created people's communes
which destroyed much of China's agriculture and industry,
reduced the nation to a state of penury and caused the deaths
of untold millions.

MAO DECIDES
The People's Republic

From 1962, with the unannounced abandonment of
Mao's plan, the economy recovered and construction of
the Beijing Subway finally began on 1 July 1965, following
another long and controversial debate about whether some
of the city's ancient walls should be demolished to make
way for it. The Chinese premier, Zhou Enlai favoured

Deng Xiaoping

preserving the walls and demolishing homes but Mao Tse-tung's voice was decisive and the homes survived, some alterations being made in the course of the construction to preserve such features of the city's fortifications as the Qianmen Gate. Mao, who presided over the Communist state from its foundation in 1949, was at the time planning the successor to the Great Leap Forward which became known as the Cultural Revolution and continued until his death in 1976. Mao's successor, Deng Xiaoping, returned the society and economy to more conventional management and began the long period of development which continues to this day. Deng himself was present to mark the start of construction work on the subway. Mao's support for the project may have been influenced by a wish for its inauguration to mark the 20th anniversary of the People's Republic, an aim which was achieved when trial services began on 1 October 1969 with services between Beijing railway station and Gongzhufen, a distance of 10.7 km (6.6 miles) serving 10 stations. This line is now incorporated in Lines 1 and 2 of the present system. Full services began in January 1971, the first underground railway in mainland China, which was initially placed under the management of the People's Liberation Army. However, politics occasionally intervened. In the period 1971–5, during the Cultural Revolution, there were 398 occasions when the Beijing Subway was closed for what were described as 'political reasons', leaving a bewildered population dependent upon its bicycles. Responsibility for the management of the subway was passed to the Beijing municipal authorities in

1975 where it has remained subject to the usual hazards of railway operation but free of political dogma.

Gongzhufen station

Olympic impetus

Until 2002 there were only two lines to serve the 21 million population, but in that year, following Beijing's successful bid for the 2008 Olympics, there began a rapid increase in the size of the network to its present size. Further extensions, with automatic, driverless operation, will add another 308 km (191.3 miles) of track bringing the total to 998 km (620.1 miles), the largest in the world.

Berlin U-Bahn

OLDEST AND BIGGEST

Berlin, long the capital of Prussia, became in 1871 capital of the new German Empire. At the end of World War II, it found itself in the middle of East Germany, under the control of the Soviet Union, its administration eventually divided between East Berlin, in the Russian zone and West Berlin, administered by the USA, Great Britain and France while the political capital of West Germany moved to Bonn. Following the fall of the Berlin Wall in 1989 Berlin resumed its role as the capital of the reunited nation of Germany. With a population of 3.6 million it is Germany's largest city and of the four underground railways in Germany (the others are at Hamburg, Munich and Nuremberg) the Berlin U-Bahn, an abbreviation for U*ntergrundbahn*, is the oldest and largest. Opened in 1902 it has 157 km (97.5 miles) of track, 9 lines numbered U1 – U9, 173 stations, carries 1.5 million passengers a day and about 560 million a year. It runs on standard gauge track, drawing 750 volts DC from a third rail. 80 per cent of the network is actually underground, mostly in sub-surface concrete shells built in the soft, sandy soil on which Berlin lies.

EARLY DAYS
Gros und Klein

Berlin Alexanderplatz station

The early lines, opened in 1902, ran East to West, serving the more affluent areas of the City but as the city expanded with the annexation of the surrounding areas, the need arose for a line to link the North of the City with the South, the latter being the future site of Tempelhof airport. For these lines it was decided that rolling stock with wider carriages should be adopted to accommodate a greater number of passengers which led to the curious distinction between the original *Kleinprofil* carriages and the later *Grosprofil* design.

The first *Kleinprofil* trains, whose design was based on Berlin's tramways, are 2.3 metres (7.5 feet) wide while the later *Grosprofil* trains designed for the North-South lines are 2.65 metres (8.6 feet) wide. London's sub-surface lines have rolling stock with more headroom than the deeper Tube lines but while the London trains have more headroom, they do not increase the passenger capacity as the *Grosprofil* carriages of the U-Bahn do.

BOARD FOR FLOWERPOTS
Mind the gap

Construction of the North-South *Grosprofil* lines began in 1912 but was interrupted by World War I. The economic consequences of the war meant that in the years that followed, the city struggled to complete the work or afford the new *Grosprofil* rolling stock. When the line opened on 30 January 1923 it had to borrow *Kleinprofil* trains from the earlier lines. The track gauge and the electrical mechanism were compatible but the new stations had been built to accommodate the wider trains, with larger gaps between the carriages and the platforms into which unwary passengers were in danger of falling. Wooden planks were provided to bridge the gap, these becoming known as *Blumenbretter*, or 'Flowerpot boards'. The eventual supply of *Grosprofil* stock removed the necessity for these encumbrances.

★ AMAZING FACT ★

WORLD WAR II
Albert Speer, later Hitler's Minister of Armaments and War Production, later imprisoned at Nuremberg for 20 years, devised a number of ambitious schemes to expand and upgrade the U-Bahn but nothing of consequence had been achieved when the war began. The stations, like those of London, were used as air raid shelters during the war and the network was extensively damaged by RAF bombing.

EXTRAORDINARY FACT

Post-war reconstruction

The division of the city into Soviet, British, American and French sectors after 1945 was followed by extensive reconstruction of the U-Bahn which was completed by 1950. Citizens could travel reasonably freely throughout the network though from 1953 loudspeakers on the trains warned passengers when the trains were about to enter the eastern sector. The U-Bahn became a popular means by which East Germans could flee to the West. Further lines were built but the construction of the Berlin Wall in August 1961 effectively divided the city, and with it the U-Bahn, into two segments. Some trains continued to run through both sectors on the U2 line but did not stop for passengers at stations in the eastern sector. These became known as Geisterbahnhofe, or 'Ghost Stations' and were patrolled by East German border guards.

Berlin, Alexanderplatz, U-Bahn-Station

QUICK FACTS

FARES The U-Bahn fares are managed in conjunction with the Berlin S-Bahn which includes the suburban rail services to the surrounding districts including Potsdam. A zonal fare system is in use, similar to that of London, with three zones. Zone A covers central Berlin; zone B is the remainder of the U-Bahn; zone Z extends to the surrounding area. A ticket for one day's travel covering all three zones is €3.6, about £3.25 at present exchange rates with concessions for pensioners, children and those with disabilities.

THE FUTURE
ON THE DRAWING BOARD

The extensive reconstruction of the city which followed the fall of the Berlin Wall has for the moment exhausted the city's appetite for major investment in the U-Bahn apart from some improvements to connections between lines and stations There are competing demands also from the S-Bahn and the city's network of tramways. Expansion plans are likely to remain on the drawing board for the immediate future.

Budapest Metro

OLDEST IN CONTINENTAL EUROPE

The Hungarian capital, Budapest, formed of two cities, Buda and Pest, on either side of the Danube, has the oldest underground railway in continental Europe.

WORLD HERITAGE SITE
Franz Joseph Electric Underground Railway

It is now 38 km in length and carries over 400 million passengers a year in a city whose population is 1.7 million. Founded in 1896, its first line entered service in May, just before that of Glasgow which opened in December the same year so Budapest's Line 1, named a World Heritage site in 2002, is pre-dated only by London's Underground. It was named the 'Franz Joseph Electric Underground Railway' and ran roughly North–South beneath Andrassy Avenue, Budapest's principal thoroughfare, for 5 km (3.1 miles) from Vorosmarty Square to Szechenyi, serving eight stations which are still in use and to which three more were added in the 1980s and 1990s. The line was built to convey passengers from the City Centre to the Budapest City Park on the occasion of the World's Fair without disfiguring the elegant lines of Andrassy Avenue.

Line 1 beneath Andrassy Avenue

Franz-Joseph I (1830–1916) was the last Emperor to rule over the Austro-Hungarian Empire. Crowned King of Austria in 1848 and of Hungary in 1967 his attempt to hold together his ramshackle empire, which extended into the Balkans, helped to bring about World War I and his death in 1916, during that conflict, ended both his dynasty and his empire. The naming of the Budapest Line 1 in his honour may be taken as a last act of homage.

THE 'HUNGARIAN PRINCIPALITY'
ROLLING INTO PICCADILLY

The Fair itself was planned to mark the 1,000th anniversary of the foundation of the 'Hungarian Principality' in 896, forerunner of the Kingdom of Hungary. The park later became the site of a circus, funfair and lido. The line was electrified from its first days and built just beneath the surface by the Cut and Cover method beneath Andrassy Avenue, still one of the capital's principal streets and itself part of the Unesco World Heritage Site. The Hungarians soon developed their own manufacturing facilities for underground electric trains and by 1906 were able to supply much of the mechanism of 216 cars for London's Piccadilly Line, the Hungarian rolling stock remaining in service in London until 1930.

A FOOTBALLER AND A NATIONAL HERO
The emergence of Hungary

Following the destruction visited upon the city in the last months of World War II and the occupation of Hungary by Russian forces, plans were drawn up with Russian engineers for an East–West line running east to what is now the Ferenc Puskás stadium (formerly called 'People's Stadium'), named after the famous Hungarian footballer; and west via Kossuth station beneath the Danube towards Moscow Square (now Széll Kálmán Square) and to a main line railway station. The name changes that stations have undergone reflect the emergence of Hungary from Soviet occupation since 1989. Construction began after many delays in the 1960s and it began to enter service in the 1970s, linked with the original line at Deak Square, the major transport and entertainment hub of Budapest. Unlike the original Line 1 it was built as a deep tube and to the utilitarian designs of the Moscow Metro. The Budapest Metro now consists of four lines, each denoted by its own colour, with 52 stations conveying an annual total of about 410 million passengers. Line 4 was inaugurated by Prime Minister Viktor Orbán in March 2014, the first fully automatic line in Hungary. A fifth line is planned.

★ AMAZING FACT ★

Ferenc Puskás (1927–2006) is remembered in Hungary as a national hero and by followers of English football with both bitterness and gratitude. He was the outstanding player of his generation and led his Hungarian team, The Mighty Magyars to victory over England by 6 – 3 at Wembley in 1953, the first home defeat by a foreign team. In Budapest later that year England were humiliated by a score of 7 – 1. This led to a shake-up in the management of English football which previously thought itself invincible. Puskas left Hungary after the failed uprising against the Communist regime in 1956 and joined Real Madrid, returning to Hungary in 1981.

EXTRAORDINARY FACT

Lajos Kossuth (1802–94) was a Hungarian lawyer and statesman who led his country as Governor-President during the uprising against Austrian rule in 1848, a period of turbulence throughout Europe. Following the intervention of Tsar Nicholas I of Russia his government was overthrown and, despite widespread popular support throughout Europe, Kossuth fled and spent the rest of his life in exile, dying in Turin in 1894. He is regarded as one of Hungary's principal national heroes.

The Buenos Aires Underground

OLDEST X 3

The Buenos Aires Underground entered service
in December 1913, making it the oldest in Latin
America, the Southern Hemisphere and the Spanish
speaking world, the Madrid underground opening
in 1919. It is known as the *Subte*, an abbreviation
of *Subterraneo*. The capital of Argentina sits on the
estuary of the River Plate with a population in the city
itself of about 3 million while that of the surrounding
province, the most densely populated area of the
country, amounts to about 15 million. There are
six lines with 57 km (35.4 miles) of track and 104
stations, these picking up passengers from tramways
serving the surrounding province. Lines ACDE and H
(opened in 2007) draw their electricity from overhead
lines at 1500 v DC while Line B uses a third rail at 750
volts DC. Weekday ridership is about 1.4 million and
annual usage about 400 million passengers. Most of
the Rolling stock is British, German or American with
some manufactured in Argentina itself. Fares are very
cheap and hard to compare with those of London
because of the tendency of the Argentine Peso to
fall in value. Suffice it to say that at the present
exchange rate a flat fare on the *Subte* is less than 20p
and can be as low as 10p for regular travellers with
concessions for students, the disabled and those who
have retired. Trains used to run from 05.30 to 01.00
but in 1994 services were curtailed at 23.00.

ORIGINS
Tramways in the air?

Illustration showing the proposal for the 'Le Tellier' elevated tramway in Buenos Aires

Proposals for improvements in the city's transit system began in the 1880s, one idea being a system of aerial electrified tramways. This would have been a revolutionary scheme at the time but enterprise gave way to cost and practicality and the city decided to add further to the already dense network of surface tramways which, in the outer regions, now act as feeders for the *Subte*. The tramways, though excellent in themselves, did little to ease the congestion on the streets. In 1896 the former mayors of the City, Miguel Cane, declared that Buenos Aires needed an Underground like that of London. After many delays it was agreed in 1907 that a subterranean railway would be built and, like London's early Underground system the Buenos Aires *Subte* was built and managed by different and sometimes competing companies.

1 DECEMBER 1913
Anglo-Argentine

The first, opening on 1 December 1913, was the creation of the Anglo-Argentine Tramways Corporation and linked two of the City's most important squares, Plaza de Mayo, a traditional gathering place for demonstrations rather like Trafalgar Square, and Plaza Miserere. It comprised much of what is now Line A. The company also owned many of the city's tramways and was slow to expand the network so the Argentine government, dissatisfied that it had built only 48 metres (157.4 feet) of the present Line C to link two of the most important rail terminals, Constitución and

A train of Buenos Aires Underground's Line A, leaving Primera Junta station

Retiro, granted concessions to other companies in the 1930s before nationalizing the entire network in 1939 and passing its management to the City of Buenos Aires itself. In 1994 the network was privatized, with the lines being operated by a company called Metrovías in a somewhat uneasy partnership with the City which owns the track, stations and rolling stock. Metrovías decided to end services 2 hours earlier than previously, arguing that extra time was required to maintain and upgrade the infrastructure. This has not proved popular but petitions to Metrovías and the City Ombudsman have yielded no concessions. At the time of writing there is a proposal to open the management of the system to other concessionaires, Transport for London being a possible contender.

New lines planned are F, G and I as well as Line P, the *Premetro* which is a Tramway delivering passengers to the *Subte*.

The Chicago 'L'

GRAIN, PORK, BEEF AND COAL BENEATH THE STREETS

At the start of the 20th century, Chicago, then America's most populous city after New York, had become the major communications hub between the cities of the East Coast like New York, Washington and Boston and the Great Plains of the Midwest which fed those cities with grain, pork and beef. In the days before an effective road network it was the centre of the American railroad system, served by 28 railroad companies and accommodating more railroad terminals than any other city in the world at that time. It was becoming America's principal centre for processing meat and grain and the home of markets in those commodities and of huge food processing corporations like Armour and Kraft. It was also expanding rapidly, with building sites throwing up offices, markets, stores and warehouses. The streets were heavily congested, with trucks and horse-drawn carts conveying building materials, coal and ash to and from new and existing stores, offices and warehouses. The city was also building a unique underground railway. Most of its urban passenger railways are above ground, commonly referred to as the 'L' because they are elevated, notably the famous 'Loop' railway. The distinctive feature was to be its freight railway which enabled merchandise travel round the city and serve the railroad terminals.

TELEPHONES TO TRAINS
Chicago Subway Co.

The metro system began life less ambitiously in 1899, as a network of narrow subterranean passages to carry the telephone cables of the Illinois Telephone and Telegraph company. In 1905 it was taken over by the Illinois Tunnel Company and, in due course and after raising further finance, the Chicago Subway Company. In the same year a separate company was formed, the Chicago Warehouse and Terminal Company, whose role was to construct freight stations above ground. These would act as interchanges between potential customers and the railway beneath their feet which transported freight around the city. More importantly, the underground railway served the network of main line terminals whose lines connected with every city in the USA. The line entered service in August 1906 over a short length of track with connections to 4 main line surface terminals.

By 1914 about 97 km (60.2 miles) of railway tunnels had been constructed through the soft blue clay on which Chicago sits. The tunnels were 2.3 metres (7.5 ft) high and 1.83 metres (6 ft) wide, with a track gauge of 61 cm (2 ft) in the tunnels. The network is particularly dense in the central 'Loop' area of the city. The rails, instead of lying on sleepers, were inserted into chairs sunk in the concrete floor of the tunnels. On the busiest sections the tunnels were 4.3 metres (14.1 ft) high and 3.9 metres (12.8 ft) wide. The city authorities required that the tunnel ceilings were at least 6.9 metres (22.6 ft) beneath the surface to ensure that they were well below the pipes and cables of utilities conveying water, gas, electricity and sewage and to allow for the future

Tunnel under construction in 1902

construction of passenger subways crossing them in the future. Two such sub-surface lines were subsequently built and in fact the freight tunnels are in places as much as 12 metres (39.3 ft) beneath the surface. In 1914 the company had over 130 electric locomotives drawing power from overhead wires and over 2,500 freight cars carrying general merchandise, coal for the heating systems of the customers, debris from building sites in the rapidly expanding city and ash from boilers. A central despatcher controlled the daily movement of about 300 trains throughout the system, each train drawing 10 to 15 cars. Over 60 electric pumps ensured that the tunnels did not become flooded, Chicago lying only a few feet above the water of Lake Michigan.

BANKS TO DEPARTMENT STORES
Coal and Ash beneath the streets

By the 1930s there were 36 connections to customers such as the railroad terminals and Chicago's famous Department store Marshall Field's, later joined by several banks, including First National Bank of Chicago, large hotels, warehouses, the North Pier Terminal Company with its 2 hectares of trading and storage space and City Hall. In the early days the biggest single cargo was coal, collected from the main line terminals on the surface and delivered to customers to heat their buildings. Two specially built coal stations were served by the Chicago and Eastern Illinois Railroad and the

Chicago and Alton Railroad stations, each of them equipped with chutes which could load one of the tunnel trucks with 3 tons of coal in 2 seconds. This would be discharged from the tunnel cars into a hopper at the customer's premises from which it would be taken by conveyor belt to the customer's boiler room. Ash from the boilers would be removed by reversing this process. In addition to the direct connections to customers (similar to private sidings on surface railways), there were 4 public stations to which any company or individual could take consignments – rather like very large post offices. As with the private connections, they were equipped with elevators which brought the tunnel cars to the surface for loading or unloading and returned them to the tracks. At its heyday in the 1930s about 2,000 cars of freight were being taken daily by the company from the main line railroad terminals and about 800 cars were collected from businesses in the city for delivery to the terminals. This amounted to half a million tons of freight a year of which about half was general merchandise and the remainder was coal, ash, building materials and debris.

Freight train leaving Marshall Field & Company's basement

Paddington to Whitechapel

The system flourished until the end of World War II when the replacement of coal by gas and electricity as the fuels of choice and the construction of better urban streets allowing the passage of lorries meant that the underground railroad lost business. In 1956 the Chicago Tunnel Company became bankrupt. Attempts were made to refinance it and run it on a more limited but viable basis but in 1959 these were abandoned and the company went into liquidation. Its assets were sold at auction for $64,000. But the tunnels remain, beneath the streets of Chicago. And it did leave one legacy which survived its own demise. In 1913, following a visit to Chicago's freight railway, Britain's General Post Office drew up plans for a Post Office Railway to be built beneath the congested streets of London from Paddington to Whitechapel via the Mount Pleasant sorting office and Liverpool Street. It was built to the same gauge, 60.9 cm (two foot), as the Chicago line. It entered service in 1927 and continued to convey letters and parcels until 2003 when it was closed in favour of road transport. But like its Chicago forbear it's still there.

The 610 mm (2 foot) gauge Illinois Tunnel Company U.S. Mail car is on the platform of Grand Central Station

The London Underground

GRAND-DADDY OF THEM ALL

The London Underground is the ancestor of all the world's underground railways, which has led to 200 others, either in existence or under construction. It opened, as the Metropolitan Railway, on 10 January 1863 and 33 years passed before it was followed by two more underground railways, in Budapest and Glasgow. It is still one of the busiest networks in the world, carrying 5 million passengers a day on eleven lines along 402 km (250 miles) of track serving 270 stations. It is used by about 1.4 billion people each year. Beginning as a steam railway the trains now draw 650 volts DC from rails and it has been effectively in public ownership since 1933 though the original builders of its lines were independent companies who were often fierce rivals.

Baker Street platform, 1906

> **QUICK FACTS**
>
> **THE METRO, THE BAR AND THE CIRCLE** The expression 'Metro' to designate the world's Underground Railways was adopted from the original, the Metropolitan Railway, first by the Paris Metro. But the debt may well have been repaid. The origins of the famous Bar and Circle design adopted by the Underground in its early days are obscure but may have been inspired by an 'M' in a Circle on a Paris Metro station.

THE TUBE
Deep Down Under

The network is commonly referred to as 'The Tube' though in fact only 45 per cent of the track and platforms are subterranean, the remaining 55 per cent being on the surface, particularly in the outer reaches in Hertfordshire, Buckinghamshire and Essex. And much of the railway which is underground is built just beneath the surface by 'Cut and Cover' methods: dig a trench in the surface; install the railway; cover it over with a concrete shell. This is true of the early

City & South London Railway train 1890

Metropolitan and District Lines. The 'Tubes' are strictly the lines that were built with tunnelling shields far beneath the surface: dig a shaft; lower the tunnelling equipment into the shaft; bore the tunnel without disturbing the surface. These are the real 'Tubes', including the first, the Northern Line, opened in 1890 and the Central Line which followed in 1900.

QUICK FACTS

THE ONLY TRUE UNDERGROUND The only line which is underground throughout its length, from Walthamstow to Brixton, is the Victoria Line, officially opened by Queen Elizabeth II in March, 1969. The Waterloo & City Line, known as 'The Drain' which connects Waterloo station with Bank, is also entirely underground but did not become part of the Underground network until 1994.

False Starts: Crystal Palaces

In 1855 two rival schemes were proposed to build railways beneath or above the streets, both of them encased in glass to protect the passengers from the smells of London – sewage and smoke at that time. One of the schemes was proposed by Sir Joseph Paxton, designer of the Crystal Palace for the Great Exhibition of 1851; the other by an architect called William Moseley who is otherwise unknown to history. They were rejected on account of their monstrous cost.

EXTRAORDINARY FACT

False Starts: buses

The construction of the London Underground was prompted, as in other cities, by the need to overcome the traffic congestion in the city's streets by the horses and carts of the time. But there were several false starts.

George Shillibeer's first omnibus

In July 1829 a man called George Shillibeer introduced an omnibus service to take people from Paddington to the city but it failed (because of traffic congestion!) causing Shillibeer to flee to France to escape bankruptcy. He later restored his fortunes by converting the omnibus to a hearse.

THE BISHOPSGATE TAVERN AND THE END OF THE WORLD
Transportation for Life

In the meantime, in 1852, the solicitor to the City of London, Charles Pearson (1793–1862) called a meeting at the Bishopsgate Tavern, close to the present site of Liverpool Street Station, a traditional locale for raising money for new enterprises. Those who attended were promised 'Enormous maps' of a new 'Arcade Railway' to relieve congestion in the City. It would run below ground but open to the air down the centre of Farringdon Road, with surface traffic passing on either side along what is still one of London's widest thoroughfares. The scheme attracted widespread support, with the Great Northern Railway setting aside £170,000 to invest in the scheme which would enable its passengers to travel in comfort from its terminus at King's Cross to their offices in the city. The scheme was not without its critics. Dr Cuming, a preacher, warned that 'The forthcoming end of the world would be hastened by the construction of underground railways burrowing into the infernal regions and thereby disturbing the devil'.

A more immediate setback than the devil was a clerk of the Great Northern Railway called Leopold Redpath who embezzled the Great Northern's funds and spent them on 'the furnishings of magnificent houses and the purchasing of articles of *vertu* by one who is undergoing the penalties of the law for his conduct'. The penalties of the law for Redpath involved transportation for life to Australia where he flourished. He was the first but by no means the last crook to be involved in the history of the London Underground, as we shall see.

QUICK FACTS

THE TIMES CHANGES ITS MIND In 1861, when the line was proposed, T*he Times* declared that the scheme was 'Utopian' and compared it with 'plans for flying machines, warfare by balloons, tunnels under the channel…an insult to common sense'. When the line opened the same newspaper, with the same editor, wrote that it 'may be regarded as the great engineering triumph of the day'.

10 January 1863

Despite Dr Cuming and Leopold Redpath, the Metropolitan Railway opened on 10 January 1863, running from Bishop's Road, Paddington to Farringdon in

Trench and partially completed cut and cover tunnel close to Kings Cross station, London

the heart of the City. In the days leading up to the opening VIP trains had travelled the route conveying Rowland Hill, the postmaster general who had devised the penny post and William Gladstone, Chancellor of the Exchequer but not the Prime Minister, Lord Palmerston. He had been invited but, at the age of 79, had replied that he 'hoped to remain above ground a little longer'. He died two years later.

WHY THREE RAILS?
DEEP DOWN UNDER

The Metropolitan Railway adopted the standard track gauge of 1435mm (4 feet 8.5 in) but early illustrations show three running rails. The third rail was laid to enable the Great Western Railway (GWR) to run trains on its 2.1 metre (7 foot) gauge from Paddington to Farringdon without passengers having to change trains. The underground was popular from the first days and after a quarrel between the Metropolitan and the GWR, the latter stopped running its trains directly on to the underground lines, leaving more time for the shuttle services of the Metropolitan. With the opening of Crossrail, it will once again be possible for trains to run direct from the West Country to Farringdon after an interval of over 150 years.

METROPOLITAN MIXTURE
Steam beneath the streets

In the absence of electric power, steam engines pulled the coaches, which were indistinguishable from those of ordinary surface trains, with first class carriages for those who could afford them. The Great Western Engineer Isambard Kingdom Brunel had been consulted about the design of a locomotive for an underground railway and had pronounced that 'If you are going a very short journey you need not take your dinner with you or your corn for your horse'. He meant that, by heating bricks before the train entered the tunnel, it should be possible to store heat to generate enough steam to complete the few miles from Paddington to Farringdon. Such an engine was designed and tested on the surface but came perilously close to exploding and was abandoned.

Instead, an engine was designed by John Fowler (1817–98), engineer to the Metropolitan Railway, with a condensing pipe which conveyed steam from the engine back to the water tank, thus preventing steam from being released into the tunnels. However it did nothing for the smoke from the engines whose release into the tunnels and on to the platforms created an atmosphere which we do not need to imagine as passengers left descriptions.

In 1879 a letter to *The Times* described a journey on the Metropolitan: 'The atmosphere was so poisonous that I was almost suffocated and was assisted from the train at an intermediate station. I requested to be taken to a chemist close at hand. Without a moment's hesitation he said "Oh, I see, Metropolitan Railway" and at once poured out a wine glass full of what he designated "Metropolitan Mixture". I asked him whether he often had such cases to which he rejoined "Why, bless you Sir, we often have twenty cases a day"'. Yet in his book *The Soul of London*, the writer Ford Madox Ford wrote 'I have known a man, dying a long way from London, sigh queerly for a sight of the gush of smoke that, on a platform of the Underground, one may see escaping in great woolly clots'.

Where are the signals?

A committee set up to hear evidence about the smoky atmosphere on the Underground heard evidence from the railway management that the fumes were health-giving and that Great Portland Street Station was 'actually used as a sanatorium for men who had been afflicted with asthma and bronchial complaints'. A train driver, Mr A. Langford, testified that he enjoyed excellent health after 34 years' service but then ruined the story by declaring that 'very seldom' did the smoke render the signals invisible!

THE METROPOLITAN RAILWAY
Survivor

It is perhaps appropriate that the Metropolitan Railway, the first to be created, was also the one that survived longest as an independent company. As the other lines were gradually absorbed by an organization that came to be known as the 'Underground Group', the Metropolitan alone maintained a separate existence until 1933 when it was absorbed, rather reluctantly, by the semi-nationalized London Passenger Transport Group. Its survival owed much to its profitability which was due to its shrewdness in developing properties adjacent to its lines as it extended its lines to Hertfordshire and, in Buckinghamshire, as far as Amersham and Chesham. It thus created, and benefited from, 'Metroland' which was made famous in the poetry of John Betjeman, who placed its capital at Chorleywood.

1921 Metro-Land *booklet published London's Metropolitan Railway*

DOWN THE TUBES
The Thames Tunnel

The first deep level tube was the City and South London Railway which opened in 1890 to connect King William Street (a station now closed on the north side of London Bridge) to Stockwell, three and a half miles to the

South and on the opposite side of the Thames. It was built using a tunnelling shield, invented in 1825 by Marc Brunel, father of the more famous Isambard Brunel. It consisted of a rectangular metal frame divided into three levels, with six compartments on each level. In each compartment was a 'miner' with a pickaxe, excavating the ground ahead of him and shovelling the spoil into a wagon behind him which removed it. When each miner had excavated about a foot, the shield was moved forward and the miners started again, protected from falling debris by the shield itself. By this means the Thames Tunnel was built, the first to be built beneath a river, linking Wapping and Rotherhithe. It was the ancestor of all tunnelling shields, including the huge machines with rotating blades that have subsequently been used to build the Channel Tunnel, Crossrail and HS2.

Stylish Living at Chiltern Court

If Chorleywood was its capital, Chiltern Court was its headquarters. This fine building above Baker Street station incorporated flats ranging from ten room Mansion flats with small bedrooms for maids, to three room Bachelor flats. Early tenants included H.G. Wells, Arnold Bennett and the American artist Edward McKnight Kauffer, whose early works included a number of posters advertising the Underground Railway. The ground floor accommodated shops (Harrods turned them down) and the Chiltern Court Restaurant, seating 250 diners and including a musicians' gallery. John Betjeman set one of his poems in the Buffet.

EXTRAORDINARY FACT

Bankrupt, inventor and gaolbird

Marc Brunel (1769–1849) was born in France, fled to the USA during the French Revolution, became City Engineer to New York and came to England in 1799 and invented a typewriter, a knitting machine, a bootmaking machine and a device for making blocks to guide the ropes of the sailing ships of Nelson's Navy. The admiralty failed to pay him for this device so, bankrupt, he was sent to the King's Bench prison for debt. The admiralty paid him £5,000 when he threatened to make his blocks available to the Russians and he was released to invent the tunnelling shield.

ELECTRIC TRAINS

NO MORE SMOKE

The City and South London was the first Railway to adopt electric locomotives, steam being out of the question so far underground. The line was electrified by the Manchester firm of Mather and Platt who designed a locomotive which ran at 40.2 kph (25 mph) on 450 volts of current. To pass beneath the Thames the trains descended until they were beneath the middle of the river and then ascended to the other side. When fully laden, the little locomotives, pulling three carriages, would struggle up the incline to King William Street on the north bank or London Bridge station to the south, lights flickering. Sometimes they would reverse and take another run at it!

QUICK FACTS

LIFTS The City and South London Railway was the first to use lifts to move passengers from street level to the platforms. They were more like cupboards than modern lifts with no lighting and the

Kennington Station

domes of the stations, like the one at Kennington, were built to accommodate the lifts' winding mechanism.

EXTRAORDINARY FACT

Padded Cells and Mind Your Head

Passengers travelled in well upholstered carriages with very small windows above head height as it was feared that the sight of walls flashing by the windows at such a depth would alarm the passengers. These fears proved groundless as did the alarm that, since there was only one class of travel, costing twopence, 'Billingsgate fish fags and Smithfield butchers' would be sharing a carriage with lords and ladies. A fine of £2 for travelling on the roof of the carriage has never had to be collected from what would presumably have been a headless corpse!

LOST STATIONS: KING WILLIAM STREET King William Street, the original northern terminus of the City and South London, was replaced by Bank station in 1900 and consequently closed. It is the oldest of several stations on the network which are no longer used for their original purpose and King William Street is now used as a document store by the offices above it, Regis House. At the outbreak of war in 1914 it was suggested by newspapers that it could become a hiding place for enemy agents and explosives but a search by police revealed no Guy Fawkes figures.

THE TUPPENY TUBE
Celebrated by Gilbert & Sullivan

The next milestone in the underground's history was marked on 27 June 1900, with the opening of the Central London Railway (now the Central Line) running from Bank station (then called Cornhill) to Shepherd's Bush. Amongst the celebrities who attended the ceremonial opening by the Prince of Wales (soon to be Edward VII) was Samuel Clemens, better known as Mark Twain. A banquet was held at Shepherd's Bush station and the railway's staff were invited to help themselves to the remains of the feast. The waiters got there first so the railwaymen found that there was plenty of food but no drink – just a lot of happy, inebriated waiters. With a flat fare of twopence it became

Mark Twain

known as the 'Tuppeny Tube' and a revival shortly afterwards of Gilbert and Sullivan's opera *Patience*, which lampooned aesthetes, referred to a 'Tuppeny tube young man'.

QUICK FACTS

VORACIOUS CURIOSITY *The Daily Mail*, not always an unqualified supporter of the Underground, was enthusiastic. It wrote of 'voracious curiosity, astonished satisfaction and solid merit' and added that 'the conductor was all of aquiver of joy and pride. But there was no indecorous exhibition of emotion; every man was resolutely British'. *The Railway Times* reported that 'a person who suffered from anorexia for eighteen months suddenly developed a ravenous appetite after a single journey on the new underground electric railway'. Miraculous indeed.

DID YOU KNOW?

New Trains give the shakes

The locomotives were purchased from the USA and were much heavier and more powerful than those of the City and South London but their weight caused problems with buildings on the surface above the route which were shaken when the trains passed beneath. A 'vibration committee' was set up under Sir John Wolfe-Barry, the designer of Tower Bridge, who heard that draughtsmen in offices in Cheapside were unable to draw straight lines with their set squares. Improved suspension on the locomotives eased the problem but it did not disappear until new units were introduced many years later.

EXTRAORDINARY FACT

Nasty smells: mind the crocodile

Within a few weeks of the line opening passengers complained about unpleasant smells on the platforms. The Reverend Professor George Henson, of the Royal Horticultural Society, suggested that the smells would be removed by planting evergreen shrubs on the platforms such as holly and rhododendrons. His suggestions were quietly ignored so he never learned how his plants would have fared in the Tuppeny Tube's sunless depths. A Member of Parliament commented that the odour reminded him of a crocodile's breath without explaining how he had survived the experience of inhaling the breath of a crocodile. Perhaps the croc had just been fed! The problem was eventually solved by pumping ozonized air into the tunnels in 1911.

WOOD LANE
The moving platform

In 1908 the London Olympics and an Anglo-French Exhibition took place at White City Stadium (so called because of the whitewashed buildings). To take advantage of the traffic this would generate the Central London Railway opened a station nearby at Wood Lane, adjacent to its depot where trains were housed overnight. The constraints of the curved site meant that the platforms to accommodate the longer trains introduced in 1927 impeded the exit from the depot so a platform extension was built on wheels. It could be rolled out of the way when a train needed to leave the depot. In 1927 the station was closed and replaced by White City station, the Westfield Shopping Centre now occupying the site. The present Wood Green station on the Circle Line was opened in 2008.

Bird's eye view of the Franco-British Exhibition (1908) in London

QUICK FACTS

BRITISH MUSEUM STATION The British Museum had its own named station from 1900 on the Central London Railway between Tottenham Court Road and Chancery Lane. In 1906 Holborn station opened on the Piccadilly Line and in 1933 the Central Line was routed via Holborn station and the British Museum station closed, though its tiled walls may be glimpsed from Central line trains just West of Holborn.

The Scarlet Pimpernel

Baroness Orczy (more prosaically known as Mrs Montague Barstow) reported that she conceived the idea of her novel *The Scarlet Pimpernel*, about a mysterious hero Sir Percy Blakeney, who rescued Frenchmen from the guillotine after the Revolution, while she was queueing to buy a ticket at Tower Hill station. And she set one of her detective stories, *The Mysterious Death on the Underground Railway* on the Metropolitan Railway.

THE FORGOTTEN TUBE
Napoleon travels by tube

Rowland Hill, inventor of the Penny Post, sought an effective way to move post around London's congested streets. The Pneumatic Despatch Company, whose directors included W.H. Smith, constructed a 60.9 cm (2 feet) diameter tube from Euston to a district post office nearby, through which 30 trains a day were, in effect, blown from February 1863. It became a curiosity for visitors and Prince Jerome Napoleon, nephew of the late Emperor, was amongst those who allowed himself to be despatched along it. Finally, following a visit to Chicago's

Testing the London Pneumatic Despatch at Battersea

underground freight railway (see *Paddington to Whitechapel*) a 60.9 cm (two foot) gauge underground railway was built between Paddington and Liverpool Street, calling at eight postal stations. Its driverless trains entered service in 1927 and it closed in 2003. Its moment of fame occurred in 1954 when Brian Johnson, the cricket commentator, travelled along it with a parcel from the BBC headquarters in Portland Place.

EXTRAORDINARY FACT

The Station with its own River

Sloane Square tube station, showing the grey conduit carrying the River Westbourne

Users of Sloane Square station on the District and Circle Line rarely notice the large metal tube passing above the trains from one platform to the other and out of the station. This is the river Westbourne which rises on Hampstead Heath, surfaces in the Serpentine in Hyde Park, and passes across the station before entering the Thames at Chelsea.

THE EAST LONDON RAILWAY
USING THE THAMES TUNNEL

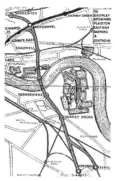

*Opened in 1869, this short line from Wapping to New Cross Gate was intended to link the mainline railways north and south of the Thames. It made use of Marc Brunel's Thames Tunnel (see **Paddington to Whitechapel**) which it thereby rescued from penury but never ran its own trains, these being supplied by the Metropolitan and District Railways to the north and components of the Southern Railway to the south. It became a link in Sir Edward Watkin's ambitious but unrealized plan for a railway from Manchester to Paris. In 1948 it passed to the London Underground and was later extended to Highbury*

1915 map of East London Railway

and Islington station to the North and Crystal Palace and West Croydon to the South. This often-forgotten corner of the network has the distinction of running through the world's oldest tunnel beneath a river.

SIR EDWARD WATKIN (1819–91)
Neasden's answer to the Eiffel Tower

Chairman of the Metropolitan Railway, Sir Edward Watkin, devised a plan to create a railway from Manchester to Paris, using companies managed by him: the Manchester, Sheffield and Lincolnshire Railway; the Great Central Railway; the Metropolitan Railway; the East London Railway; and the South-Eastern Railway; and a Channel Tunnel of which he was a persistent advocate and actually began to

Watkin Tower first stage

build. He would then link it with the French Chemin du Nord, of which he was a director, which would complete the link to Paris. When Parliament (of which he was a Member) questioned the wisdom of the tunnel on grounds of national security he gave the reassuring reply that by pressing a button on his desk he could blow it up in five minutes: hardly a comfort for passengers!

Frustrated by Parliament's censure of the Channel Tunnel he turned his energy to building a tower at Neasden in north London which would rival Paris's Eiffel Tower. It was called the Watkin Tower but never rose above the first level, attracted few visitors (Neasden is not particularly scenic) and was blown up in 1907, its site then being claimed to build Wembley Stadium.

CHARLES TYSON YERKES
Lots Road power station

Yerkes was one of several rogues without whom we would not have the London Underground. Born in Philadelphia, he served a prison sentence before being run out of Chicago following a number of swindles in setting up that city's elevated railway, 'The Loop' and came to London where he proceeded to raise money to build the Charing Cross, Euston and Hampstead Railway (later combined with the City and South London to create the Northern Line); launch what later became the Piccadilly Line; complete the Bakerloo Line; and electrify the District Line. At this point most of the network, the Underground Group, except the Metropolitan was under his management. When he died in New York in December 1905 he left these railways on the brink of bankruptcy. He left his New York mansion, collection of old masters and gold bedstead to the citizens of New York. But his numerous creditors got there first. To such men do we owe the London Underground.

Charles Tyson Yerkes

One legacy of Yerkes was the Lots Road power station in Chelsea which was built to generate electricity for the network. The riverside site was chosen because it was easily accessible by barges conveying the huge quantities of coal required for its boilers. It was converted first to oil and later to gas and closed in 2002. It was featured in a World War II poster of 'The Proud City'. It is now the site of shops, restaurants and luxury apartments in this fashionable district of London.

EXPATRIATES TO THE RESCUE
'A busy man': no more babies please!

It fell to two people from other countries to rescue the network from the disastrous financial legacy of Yerkes. The first was Sir Edgar Speyer, a banker of German origin who staved off threatened bankruptcy with money from his own bank and refinanced the various securities that Yerkes had used to raise cash from shareholders. Speyer also recruited Albert Stanley (1874–1948) who had emigrated to the USA from Derby in 1888 and rose to become general manager of the New Jersey tramways. Under his leadership the Underground Group became the dominant force in London's transport, operating trains and buses. In 1913 he re-assumed British citizenship and in 1920 became Lord Ashfield. In 1933 he became chairman of the London Passenger Transport Board which, for the first time, included all the Underground Railways including the Metropolitan Railway.

One of Lord Ashfield's more unusual commitments arose when he was invited to become godfather to Mary Ashfield Eleanor Hammond who was born to Mrs Daisy Hammond on a Bakerloo Line train on the evening of 13 May 1924. Ashfield accepted, adding 'Of course it would not do to encourage this sort of thing as I am a busy man'.

Murder on the Underground

Besides the fictional murder of Baroness Orczy, the Underground has, unfortunately, also witnessed some of the real kind. On 25 May 1957, a Polish survivor of the Ravensbruck concentration camp, Countess Teresa Lubienska, was murdered by stabbing at Gloucester Road station. The culprit was never found. On 13 July 1959, two policemen arrested Guenther Podola who was trying to blackmail a housewife from a telephone booth at South Kensington station. Podola shot dead Detective Sergeant Raymond Purdy. He was arrested, found guilty and on 5 November was the last person to be hanged for murdering a policeman. On 15 March 1976 train driver Stephen Julius, a married man from the West Indies, was shot dead by Vincent Kelly, an Irish terrorist who was carrying a bomb and whom Julius had tried to apprehend. On 9 December 1988 a tourist was stabbed to death by a mugger who was arrested and gaoled.

EXTRAORDINARY FACT

Whitaker Wright

Among the many colourful characters involved in building the London Underground, Whitaker Wright stands out. Having become a millionaire from mining in the USA, he set about building the Bakerloo Line. Despite various questionable stratagems to rescue his waning fortunes, his enterprises failed and he fled to France and then the USA to escape his creditors. Extradited from New York he was found guilty of defrauding investors to the value of £5 million and sentenced to 7 years penal servitude. Shortly afterwards he collapsed, having swallowed a cyanide capsule he had kept with him, together with a loaded revolver which was recovered from his clothing by the police. He left behind a mansion at Witley, Surrey, which included a lake which accommodated an underwater billiard hall encased in glass. It's still there! To such men do we owe the London Underground.

Whitaker Wright

SHABBY TREATMENT
Abuse of Privilege

Edgar Speyer (1862−1932) was of German ancestry, born in New York, came to London as chairman of the family bank and became a British subject in 1892. Besides rescuing the Underground Railway, he was a generous philanthropist who was an early patron of the Promenade concerts and founder of the Whitechapel art gallery. He was appointed

Pemberton Billing

to the Privy Council and made a baronet for his philanthropic work but none of this saved him from the xenophobia of an MP called Pemberton Billing who, using Parliamentary privilege, accused him (and Albert Stanley) of working for the Germans in World War I. Speyer retired to the USA and died in Germany in 1932. Stanley survived to become a cabinet minister under Lloyd George and, eventually, Lord Ashfield.

ART ON THE UNDERGROUND
Lorenzo the Magnificent

Frank Pick (1878−1941) the austere and hard-working managing director of the Underground Group under Ashfield's chairmanship, is remembered as a notable patron of the arts. He employed the modernist architect Charles Holden (1875−1960) to design stations for the Northern Line and Metroland, many of them now listed buildings. He recognized the emerging art of lithographic printing and applied it to the design of posters promoting travel by Underground, becoming the early patron of such artists as McKnight Kauffer, Mabel Lucie Attwell, Paul Nash, Graham Sutherland and Frank Brangwyn. He was described by one critic as 'The nearest approach to Lorenzo the Magnificent that a modern democracy can achieve' and the architectural historian Nikolaus Pevsner declared that Pick was 'the greatest patron of the arts whom this century has so far produced in England'. Pick also commissioned the artist Edward Johnston to design the new lettering for Underground signs and redesign the bar and circle sign. He could be scathing. He reprimanded the engineer who designed the station layout at Sudbury Town for cluttering up the platforms with automatic machines and ordered that it remain in that state 'as a permanent memorial to the department that cannot do its work properly'.

QUICK FACTS

55, BROADWAY Charles Holden's most striking Underground building is the organization's headquarters at 55, Broadway, above St James' Park station in Westminster, completed in 1929 at which date it was London's tallest office building. It featured controversial sculptures by Jacob Epstein (1880–1959) representing Day and Night and others by Eric Gill and Henry Moore. It remains one of London's most striking buildings.

Headquarters of London Underground designed by Charles Holden

'STUDYING FOREIGN RAILWAYS'
The Bauhaus

Pick gave his interests in his *Who's Who* entry as 'studying foreign railways' and he spent 17 days doing this in 1930 in the company of Charles Holden. It's not clear what Mrs Pick thought of this! It was on this trip that they became interested in the ideas of the Bauhaus school of architecture founded by Walter Gropius (1883–1969) and persecuted by the Nazis: simple geometric shapes, clear lines and colours. The listed station at Arnos Grove is a fine example.

Harry Beck (1901–74) and his map

Early Underground maps used colours to distinguish different lines but followed the geography that the lines covered. Harry Beck, a draughtsman accustomed to electrical wiring diagrams, designed a map which preserved the colours but used only straight lines and sharp angles to delineate their routes and made the distance between stations look almost uniform, reasoning that passengers didn't care how far apart stations were, only wanting to be sure they were going in the right direction. After some hesitation Pick adopted the map which proved an instant success and became a design icon, widely copied by other systems. Since Beck had not been employed by the Underground when he prepared the design, he owned the copyright. Pick offered him 5 guineas (£5.25) which Beck accepted. Reproduced on tea towels, clothing and mouse mats, it has made more money for London Transport than trains ever will!

EXTRAORDINARY FACT

Maths and Poetry on the Underground

The artistic heritage of Frank Pick endures. In 1986, Poetry on the Underground was launched, one of the first being displayed on trains being Wordsworth's *Composed upon Westminster Bridge*, beginning with the words 'Earth has not anything to show more fair' and proceeding to include poetry from mediaeval times to John Betjeman. And in 1992 this was followed by Maths on the Underground with a series of posters designed by Cambridge's Isaac Newton Institute featuring such subjects as aerodynamics and chaos theory.

THE NORTHERN LINE
Gas explosion

In 1924 the Underground Group, which by then owned most of the network, began to plan a connection between the City and South London Railway and the Charing Cross, Euston and Hampstead Railway. This required them to enlarge the tunnels of the City and South London from the original 3.05 m (10 ft 2 in) to the 3.5 m (11 ft 8 in) of the Hampstead line. A special tunnelling shield was used for the work at night which could be left in place for trains to pass through it in the daytime. All went well until 27 November 1943 when a train dislodged a plank of wood which triggered a series of accidents ending in a gas explosion and the rupturing of a water main which fortunately extinguished the resulting fire. Miraculously no-one was killed and in 1924 the two lines were connected via a junction between Camden and Euston.

This created the Northern Line which eventually ran from Morden in the South to Edgware and High Barnet in the North.

QUICK FACTS

LOST STATIONS: SOUTH KENTISH TOWN This station, between Camden Town and Kentish Town on the Northern Line, opened in 1907, was closed temporarily in 1924 but never reopened. An unlikely story about a stranded passenger gained credibility from a 1951 broadcast by John Betjeman who claimed that the lost passenger was a tax inspector who was found by a group of railway workers and told he was trespassing. How he got there, if he did, was never explained. The station later became a pawnbroker and massage parlour and remains a rather unattractive feature of Kentish Town Road, prone to attacks by graffiti artists.

DID YOU KNOW?

Underground Alcohol

One of the lesser-known facilities of the Underground was that for many years some of its stations had licensed premises which were able to serve alcohol when the pubs were closed. 'Pat Mac's Drinking Den' on the eastbound Metropolitan line platform at Liverpool Street station survived until 1978 when it became a café. The one on the eastbound platform at Sloane Square thrived until 1985 and enjoyed brief literary celebrity in Evelyn Waugh's 1930 novel *Vile Bodies* when Mr Chatterbox, gossip columnist for the *Daily Excess* (a scarcely disguised *Daily Express*) reported that 'the buffet at Sloane Square tube station had become the haunt of the most modern artistic coterie'.

EXTRAORDINARY FACT

Rolling Stock

The 'Padded Cells' of the City and South London and the more conventional stock of the Central were both equipped with gates at the end of the carriage to board and alight. A guard in each carriage opened and closed these and indicated to the driver by hand signals that it was safe to depart. In 1919 the Underground Group ordered from Cammell Laird in Birkenhead forty carriages with air operated doors, reducing the need for staff and these were the model for the future. Electric motors mounted in the units dispensed with the need for locomotives and when the motors were located beneath the carriages this left more space for passengers.

Lost Stations: Down Street

Down Street station, between Hyde Park Corner and Green Park, on the Piccadilly Line, was closed in 1932 for lack of passengers and in 1939 it was fitted out with offices for emergency use. It was used during the war by the Railway Executive Committee and occasionally by the War Cabinet. It is now a convenience store in the heart of Mayfair, conspicuous by virtue of the dark red tiling used for many of the Yerkes stations.

EXTRAORDINARY FACT

Underground on the Isle of Wight

In 1966 the Chief Mechanical and Electrical Engineer of the Southern Region of British Rail told the General Manager, David McKenna, that the trains on the Isle of Wight Railway, some of which dated from the reign of Queen Victoria, had reached the end of their lives. The railway was essential for taking children to school and holidaymakers from Ryde pier head to holiday destinations in Sandown and Shanklin. The tunnels and bridges on the line ruled out the use of trains from the main line railway so 43 units of 1938 Northern Line stock were bought from London Underground and adapted for use on the Island Line. They

entered service in March 1967 and in December 2019 replacement units were ordered dating from the 1970s. The Island, with its 50-year-old stock, regularly heads the league tables for punctuality.

1938 rolling stock

QUICK FACTS

GHOSTLY APPARITIONS Several station staff at Covent Garden have claimed to see a slim, six-foot-tall man, in a grey suit wearing white spectacles and one porter requested a transfer to another station having seen him. There have been persistent stories of night maintenance staff hearing running feet at Elephant and Castle and in 1968 workmen building the new Victoria Line near Vauxhall Station reported seeing a ghost seven feet tall whom they called 'The Quare fellow'.

Escalators

The network's first escalator was installed at Earl's Court station in October 1911, following one at the nearby exhibition centre which had been in place for some years. On its first day a one-legged man called Bumper Harris was seen using the escalator by reporters and a story emerged that he was being paid by the management of the Underground to do this in order to reassure passengers as to its safety. Alas this was not so.

FRANK PICK VS CHURCHILL
A German model

Frank Pick was seconded to the Ministry of Information during World War II. As war approached Pick had been asked to help with the design of posters to recruit women to join what became the Women's Royal Voluntary Service. He asked his young assistant, Anthony Bull, to find a suitable model for the posters: a woman attractive and resolute rather than glamorous. This task completed, and the posters produced, it was discovered (but not revealed) that the young woman was German!

Pick fell out with Winston Churchill over some leaflets which spread false information when dropped over Germany. When Pick told Churchill that he had never told a lie Churchill replied: 'This afternoon I shall be

Churchill

visiting Dover. I may be killed by a German shell from their long range guns. It will be a great comfort to me to know that on the last day of my life I spoke with a man who had never told a lie. Get out'. That was Pick's final contribution to the war effort.

'PADDOCK'
The station that never was

North End station, on the Northern Line between Hampstead and Golders Green, was built in the hope that dwellings would spring up in the area but this was frustrated by prohibitions on the development of nearby Hampstead Heath. The station was never opened but was turned into what Winston Churchill in his war memoirs described as 'A citadel for the War Cabinet near

Mysterious Structures

During World War II, large underground refuges were built adjacent to seven stations on the Northern Line and one at Chancery Lane. They were built as deep shelters for use by government in the event of London becoming uninhabitable under bombardment. They still exist and are recognizable for the large modernist brick structures on the surface, sometimes whitewashed. The most conspicuous is now called the Eisenhower Centre, near Goodge Street Station, so called because it was the communications centre for the D-Day invasion on 6 June, 1944, where the first news was received of the landings on the beaches.

Hampstead with offices and bedrooms and wired and fortified telecommunications'. A man who was on Home Guard duty at the station in 1940 was alarmed 'when Mr Churchill popped out of the ground at my feet'. The exit Churchill used is still there, with a notice stating that it is an electrical installation. It is in fact an emergency exit for engineers working on the track.

QUICK FACTS

THE EMPIRE WINDRUSH The passengers on the HMT *Empire Windrush* which brought the first West Indian immigrants to London in June 1948, were first housed in the Clapham Common deep shelter and in the days that followed they sought employment at the nearest employment exchange in Coldharbour Lane, Brixton. Thus was born the Afro-Caribbean community of Brixton.

EXTRAORDINARY FACT

Sheltering on the Underground

During World War I some Underground stations had been used as air raid shelters. As war approached again in 1939 the government announced that in any future conflict this would be forbidden. The population of London decided otherwise at Liverpool Street station when, on 8 September 1940 at the height of the Battle of Britain, a huge crowd forced themselves past the hapless Home Guard who were posted to keep them out. The Underground shelters quickly became a feature of life during the Blitz with special trains called Tube Refreshment Specials supplying hot food and drink; concerts; darts contests between shelters and plays. 36 doctors and 200 nurses set up medical posts to attend to the sick and babies were born in the shelters.

WAR FACTORIES
73 London Transport Spitfires

The Underground made its contribution to World War II in more direct ways. Staff raised money for two Spitfires which went into battle with RAF roundels on the wings and the London Transport bar and circle on the fuselage. At Acton rolling stock depot Sherman tanks were converted to 'Swimming tanks' for the invasion of Normandy and the crossing of the Rhine. An 8-km (5-mile) section of the uncompleted Central Line between Leytonstone and Gants Hill were converted into an aircraft components factory for the Plessey company and the subway linking South Kensington station with the museums was used for making aircraft components, the work being done by London Transport employees in their free time.

★ AMAZING FACT ★

THE MOORGATE DISASTER

On 28 February 1975 occurred the worst disaster in the history of the network at Moorgate Station in the heart of the City when a Northern Line train with an experienced driver, Leslie Newson, at the controls crashed into the concrete wall at the end of the platform at 64 kph (40 mph). 43 people were killed and 74 injured. It took police, fire and rescue and ambulance staff four days to remove the dead and injured. No convincing explanation of the accident could be identified. The train was in good condition and the driver a sensible, experienced man in good health. It remains a mystery.

Crossrail: Main Lines Beneath London

BACK TO BRUNEL AND THE GWR

As observed in *The London Underground*, for a few months in 1863 it was possible to travel on a Great Western train from Reading to Farringdon, using the tracks of the Metropolitan Railway for the final stage of the journey from Paddington to its destination at Farringdon in the heart of the City. 160 years later it will again be possible thanks to *Crossrail* which, upon its opening, will be known as the *Elizabeth Line*. How appropriate it is that two of the Tunnel Boring machines that have been creating the tunnels are named after Isambard Kingdom Brunel's mother and wife.

THE ROUTE
Confidence or impudence?

In June, 1941, at the height of the war when the future of the kingdom hung by a thread, a railwayman called George Dow wrote an article for the London Evening Newspaper *The Star*, proposing the construction of a main line railway beneath the streets of the capital. Was this confidence or impudence to make such a proposal at a time of national peril? Many years of planning followed as schemes were devised, considered, abandoned and redrafted before the first tunnels began to be bored in May, 2012.

The route chosen serves 40 stations from Reading and Heathrow in the West to Shenfield in Essex and Abbey Wood

in Kent, a distance of approximately 120 km (74.5 miles).
There are Portals, or entry points for the tunnels at:
Royal Oak, West of Paddington.
Pudding Mill Lane, E 16, near the Olympic Park.
Plumstead in the Borough of Greenwich.
North Woolwich, south of London City airport.
Victoria Dock in the London Borough of Newham.
Through central London the line passes through seven
stations, each of which has been expanded and decorated by
artists from Great Britain, France and the USA. These are at
Paddington, Bond Street, Tottenham Court Road, Farringdon,
Liverpool Street, Whitechapel and Canary Wharf.

THE TUNNEL BORING MACHINES (TBMS)
Homage to iconic women

The TBMs, descendants of Marc Brunel's original
tunnelling shield, are in effect large factories, operating
round the clock with crews of 20 at a time. Rotating knives
cut through the tunnel face and the spoil thus generated is
deposited on a conveyor belt and taken away for disposal. The
TBMs, working in pairs on the parallel tunnels, are all named
after women:

Victoria and Elizabeth; the queens in whose reigns the first
and most recent lines have been built.

Ada and Phyllis; Ada Lovelace, daughter of Lord Byron
and computer pioneer; and Phyllis Pearsall, designer of the
Geographers' A–Z Map Company.

Sophia and Mary; Sophia Kingdom, wife of Marc and

mother of Isambard Kingdom Brunel; and Mary Brunel, wife of Isambard; mother- and daughter-in-law working in tandem.
Jessica and Ellie: Olympic and Paralympic champions Jessica Ennis–Hill and Ellie Simmonds.

Marc Brunel's original tunnelling shield

Tunnelling was completed on 4 June 2015 when Victoria broke though the last segment of London clay to be greeted by PM David Cameron and Mayor Boris Johnson at Farringdon station.

The Eye of the Needle

One of the most nerve-wracking engineering challenges faced by the engineers involved boring a tunnel through Tottenham Court Road station, 30 cm (12 in) below a pair of escalators and 91 cm (36 in) above Northern Line platforms. The engineers looked confident throughout this delicate operation but surely they must have felt some tremors?!

QUICK FACTS

TRAINS AND SIGNALS The trains, built by Bombardier at their Derby works, will draw current from overhead wires at 25kvs, unlike the rest of the Underground network which works on 3rd rail 650 kv DC. Within the tunnels Crossrail will be guided by a signalling system similar to the 'moving block' used on parts of the New York subway, with the speed of the trains governed by the distance from the train ahead.

A new nature reserve

7 million tons of debris has been generated by Crossrail. Much of it has been removed from the site by Thames barges to Wallasea Island which lies close to the mouth of the River Crouch in Essex before it joins the North Sea. In its long history, dating from Roman times and earlier it has been used for grazing and for growing wheat on silt deposited at the end of the last Ice Age. It has at times supported a few inhabitants but is subject to flooding by seawater despite its seawall which is being demolished to create a wetland nature reserve to accommodate Brent Geese, wigeon, curlew and fish like herring, bass and flounder – the largest man-made nature reserve in Europe.

★ AMAZING FACT ★

Money Troubles
The original budget for Crossrail was £14 billion with an opening date of December 2018 but shortly before the planned opening it was announced that it would be postponed. An opening date of 2022 is now anticipated with a likely eventual cost closer to £19 billion. The reasons for delay and overspend are not entirely clear but difficulties with reconciling the signalling system in the tunnels with that on the surface appear to be one; and, more surprisingly, finishing the stations in the tunnels. Watch this space.

EXTRAORDINARY FACT

Woolly Mammoths and skulls

The Crossrail excavations proved a rich source of relics for archaeologists, including the jawbone of a woolly Mammoth, a large piece of amber (which is now in the Natural History Museum) and more than 50 human skulls, with no bodies attached, from the vicinity of Liverpool Street station. They date from the Roman era and may be from the time that Boudicca sacked London in about 60 AD or from a later rebellion against the Emperor Hadrian in about 125 AD.

The Madrid Metro

Spain's capital, with a population of 3.2 million, is also its largest city. It was one of the first cities on the European continent to have an underground railway whose construction was facilitated by the light clay and sand soil on which it stands. On 17 October 1919 Spain's King Alfonso XIII took an inaugural ride on Madrid's new Metro. The trip was a short one though, the line being only 3.4 km (2.1 miles) long including eight stations and running from Puerta del Sol to Cuatro Caminos. Two days later, on 19 October, the line was opened to the public and was immediately popular. The network now comprises 293 km (182 miles) of track laid to the unusual 1445 mm gauge (4 ft 8 ⅞ in) (1 cm greater than standard gauge) with twelve lines, numbered 1 to 12, serving 302 stations, an average of only 800 metres (2,624 feet) apart. Virtually the entire system is underground, with only eight surface stations, the remainder being just below the surface. In addition, four Metro Ligero (light rail) lines, laid to standard gauge, and partly on the surface, serve as feeders to the Metro. Owned and run by private enterprise in its early days, the network is now managed by a public corporation, Metro de Madrid. Fares are based on eight zones of which the outer zones stretch well into the suburbs. A fare within one zone costs €1.50 cents, about £1.40, with discounts for multiple use tickets, children and pensioners.

NOT TOO FAR TO WALK
Iberian Gauge

With an average distance between stations of 800 metres (2,624 feet), and less than that in the central area, the Madrid Metro is one of the densest networks in Europe, the aim being to put stations within a short walk for pedestrians. The early signalling system was such that a train could not depart from one station until the one ahead was vacated by the preceding train.

QUICK FACTS

IBERIAN GAUGE The choice of standard 1435 mm (4 ft 8.5 in) gauge. track for the Metro Ligero is made more peculiar by the fact that Spanish surface rail tracks are laid to the Iberian Gauge of 1668 mm (about 5 feet 5.6 in) thus giving Spain 3 track gauges – Iberian, Metro and Standard gauge!

TRACTION
HOW MANY VOLTS?

The entire system was electrified from the early days using overhead supply. Five lines draw 600 volts DC; the Metro Ligero draws 750 volts DC; and the remainder 1500 volts DC. In 1999 the Metro began to install a new patented system for its electricity supply in the form of a solid rail suspended from the ceiling of the tunnels, a more robust system than the conventional wires hung from gantries.

QUICK FACTS

KEEP LEFT Unusually, Madrid Metro trains run on the left rather than the right, the reason being that, until 1924, road vehicles kept to the left, as in Britain, unlike most of the continent of Europe. The later lines which followed the road traffic switch continued to follow the 'keep left' rule.

Left or Right? Caesar or Napoleon?

Roman armies kept to the left on the roads they built. Napoleon Bonaparte' armies, following the French Revolution, marched on the right to emphasize their revolutionary credentials, a rule followed by those nations which had the doubtful pleasure of being occupied by them. Those which escaped such as Britain, Ireland and Sweden (until 1972, see the *Stockholm Underground*) continued to drive on the left. Spain was invaded by the French but never subdued and the French were driven out by the armies of the future Duke of Wellington.

BY ROYAL SUBSCRIPTION
An ungrateful nation

Three engineers — Miguel Otamendi, Carlos Mendoza, and Antonio González Echarte, who had visited the USA in 1904 and studied urban transport systems, put forward a proposal for the construction of the first Madrid underground line in 1914 and royal permission was granted provided that they could raise the 8 million pesetas required. 4 million was put up by a Spanish Bank on condition that the remainder was raised from shareholders. When 2.5 million pesetas had been raised from that source the king himself subscribed the balance of 1.5 million pesetas so it was appropriate that Alfonso XIII, the line's largest shareholder, took the first train ride and officially opened it.

Having shown their appreciation of the Metro which Alfonso XIII had helped to create, his faithless subjects proceeded to replace him with a Republican regime. Alfonso had been king from the day of his birth in 1886 since his father had died the previous year. Following a Regency presided over by his mother, Alfonso took up the reins of power in 1902 at the age of 16 but went into voluntary exile in 1931 following elections which clearly showed a desire to abolish the monarchy. He died in Rome in 1941 by which time the turbulence which followed his exile had been ended by the dictatorship of General Franco. The present king of Spain, Felipe VI, born in 1968, is his great grandson.

EXTRAORDINARY FACT

Steady Growth

The popularity and financial success of the Metro was evident from its early days. Over 43,000 passengers a day in its first three months of operation paid enough in fares to enable investors to raise 12 million further pesetas to be raised from investors and the network has grown steadily, with interruptions during the Spanish Civil War and World War II. Expansion accelerated in the 1970s as Spain started to earn substantial sums of foreign exchange from tourism and as its capital became a popular destination for foreign visitors. The Puerta del Sol, the great square in the centre of Madrid, became the centre of the Metro network as it always had been of Madrid's Road Network.

WIDE AND NARROW ROLLING STOCK
A question of width

One of the peculiarities of the Madrid Metro is its rolling stock, which comes in two widths. In the early days of the Metro, and as a matter of policy under the Franco dictatorship, the trains of the Madrid Metro were built only by the Spanish company Construcciones y Auxiliar de Ferrocarriles (CAF) who in 2019 won a contract to supply new trains for London's Docklands Light Railway. More recently, the Italian company Ansaldo Breda, a subsidiary of the Japanese Hitachi corporation, has supplied trains for Madrid from its base in Naples. The platforms of the early stations were 60 metres (196.8 feet) long and could accommodate only 4-car trains 2.3 metres (7.5 feet) in width but some stations have been extended and the more recent lines, dating from the 1970s, have platforms of 90 to 115 metres (295.2 to 492.1 feet). When the new line 7 was opened in 1974 it was designed to take trains 2.8 metres (9.1 feet) wide and this has now become the standard size.

The future

Expansion plans were halted by the 2008 financial crash which had particularly dire effects upon Spain and, more recently, by the collapse of tourism following the Covid 19 pandemic. Some improvements have been made to facilities to give disabled passengers access to the network and there is a plan to extend line 5 to Barajas, Madrid's main International airport.

Mexico City Metro

BIGGEST CITY IN THE AMERICAS

Mexico's capital, with its population of almost 22 million, is the most populous city in the Americas where only the New York Subway is more heavily used than the *Metro de la Ciudad de Mexico*. It has a daily ridership of 4.5 million and annual total of 1.7 billion. It has 227 km (141 miles) of tracks at standard 1435 mm (4 ft 8.5 in) gauge, 195 stations and twelve lines. Ten of the lines use rolling stock with pneumatic rubber tires, like those in use on the Paris Métro. They are quieter than steel and better suited to the unstable ground within which the lines are built. 115 stations are underground, 54 on the surface and 26 are elevated. A single ticket for one trip costs at the present rate of exchange about 15 pence, with free travel for the elderly, accompanied children under 5 and those with disabilities. There are 14 types of standard gauge rolling stock from France (Alstom), Canada (Bombardier) Spain (CAF) and Concarril of Mexico. Electricity is drawn from overhead pantographs at 1500v. It is the highest system in the world above sea level and entered service on 4 September 1969. Its official name is *Sistema de Transporte Colectivo* and is commonly referred to as STC.

A MOUNTAIN CITY IN A LAKE
Being put to the test

By the 1950s the highways in the centre of the city were so congested that traffic struggled to match walking pace. The city is at an elevation of 2,286 metres (7,500 feet) and in an area subject to earthquakes. Moreover the city itself is built above an ancient shallow lake whose sediments magnify the shocks from any movement of the ground. This raised doubts about the wisdom and feasibility of building beneath the unstable surface which made the tunnels relatively easy to bore but required a design which would withstand earthquake shocks. A rectangular rather than circular design for the tunnels was proposed as being most appropriate and work began on 19 June 1967.

The engineers' design was put to the test on the morning of 19 September 1985, sixteen years after the first line was built, when a massive earthquake devastated the city, but not the Metro. At 8.1 on the Richter scale the tremor was even greater than the 7.9 quake which destroyed San Francisco in 1906. The Metro was briefly closed to facilitate rescue work and clearing of debris on the surface but it passed the test. It survived intact.

QUICK FACTS

A MAMMOTH AND AN AZTEC IDOL Much of the system is built just below the surface and the tunnellers unearthed over 20,000 objects of interest to archaeologists including a sculpture of the Aztec goddess Coatlicue, the bones of a Woolly Mammoth (now exhibited at Talisman station) and an altar to the Aztec god Ehecatl, now on show at Pino Suárez station.

Expansion

Expansion of the system followed quickly from the first line and was not interrupted by the earthquake which was taken as evidence that the city was suited to an underground railway. At intervals of about five years new lines have been added, with construction of number twelve beginning in 2008 and the terminal following in 2015.

STATIONS AND HEROES
WHAT'S IN A NAME

Rather than naming stations after the districts that they serve, they are often named after people and events from Mexico's often turbulent history, many of those honoured meeting early and violent deaths. Thus one station, Zapata, owes its name to Emiliano Zapata (1879–1919), leader of a peasant rebellion in the years after 1910 which led to a new constitution of 1917 (itself the name of a station, (Constitucion de 1917). Zapata was assassinated in 1919 and is consequently memorialized by a station as well as a moustache. Another leader, Pancho Villa (1878–1923), another victim of the assassin's bullet, has not been honoured by a station name but by the army he led, with limited success, in the station name Division del Norte. A more familiar name is that of Garibaldi station: not the hero of Italian unity but his grandson, Peppino Garibaldi (1879–1950) who, besides the Mexican revolution, participated in four other wars in four nations before dying peacefully in Rome in 1950. War was the family business.

The Moscow Metro

BUSIEST IN EUROPE DESPITE THE PATRIARCH

The Moscow Metro is the busiest underground railway in Europe, carrying 2.5 billion passengers each year and as many as 9.7 million on its busiest day – numbers exceeded only by systems built more recently in the Far East. It has 15 lines, 264 stations and 462 km (287 miles) of track, the longest outside China. Its tracks are laid to the Russian 1520 mm (5 foot) gauge and trains are powered by 825 v. DC current drawn from a third rail except for lines 13 and 14 which draw 3 kv DC from overhead catenaries. It opened in 1935, though the idea of an underground railway for Moscow can be traced back to the Tsarist era when the City Council first put forward plans in 1900. The plans were effectively vetoed by a combination of the Imperial Archaeological Office and the Patriarch of Moscow who both objected that the tunnels would undermine the foundations of the Kremlin and a number of Russian Orthodox Churches. Such considerations did not concern Josef Stalin.

MOSCOW
The Bolshevik Capital

The capital of Russia in Tsarist times had been St Petersburg since the reign of Peter the Great (1672–1725) who had carved the city out of the Baltic Sea and the Neva River. The Bolsheviks, who seized power in 1917, moved the capital to Moscow and the centre of power to the Kremlin, (the word means 'citadel'). Many other buildings of note in Moscow had been destroyed by the fire of 1812 during Napoleon's disastrous occupation of the city in his failed invasion of Russia.

On 21 March 1933 the Soviet Government set out a plan for ten lines, each of them quite short, with a total length of 80 km (49.7 miles). The absence of many ancient buildings enabled the designers of the Metro to embark upon an ambitious radial plan for the network, with thirteen lines running across the city to all points of the compass, linked by the 20 km (12.4 mile) *Koltsevaya* ('Circle' Line) at a short distance from the hub of the system which is the Kremlin itself. This was built in 1950 and in 2016 a further and bizarrely named 'Moscow Central Circle', at a greater distance, from the centre, and 54 km (33.5 miles) long, was added.

LAZAR KAGANOVICH
The Iron Commissar

The task of executing the plan was entrusted to Lazar Kaganovich (1893–1991) a fanatical supporter of Stalin. Born in 1893 to a Jewish family in Ukraine, he had helped to secure Stalin the post of General Secretary of the Communist Party in succession to Lenin in 1922. Kaganovich remained an unquestioning supporter of Stalin and once declared publicly that he would carry out any order given to him by the dictator. He became known as 'The Iron Commissar' and was Stalin's idea of a manager, which ensured his survival throughout and beyond the Stalinist era, dying in 1991 at the

Lazar Kaganovich

age of 1997, the last of the old Bolsheviks. Nikita Khrushchev, Stalin's eventual successor, was appointed to assist Kaganovich in his work on the Metro, an appointment attributed by Khrushchev in his memoirs to the fact that he had experience of the mining industry. The Moscow Metro was actually named after its creator, known as the *Metropolitan Kaganovich*, until the Khrushchev era in 1955 when the new leader decided that Kaganovich belonged to the past.

THE UKRAINIAN GENOCIDE
'We are trying to make an omelette'

The construction of the Metro was part of Stalin's second Five Year Plan which, between 1928 and 1938, was intended to turn the Soviet Union from a rural peasant economy into a modern industrial power. To promote the construction of the first stage of the Metro Kaganovich was also appointed by Stalin to the key post of Minister of Heavy Industry. To these ends the agricultural sector was ruthlessly co-opted, with the intention to increase productivity and to enable agricultural produce to be exported in exchange for machinery and raw materials imported from the West to support Russia's industrialisation. The result was the great famine of 1932−33, known as the *Holodomor* and what amounted to genocide amongst rural communities, especially in the rich agricultural area of the Ukraine where Kaganovich was born. It is estimated that between 5 and 7 million people died from the famine. In January 2010 the Court of the Ukraine, now an independent state, found Kaganovich posthumously guilty of genocide during the *Holodomor* and the Great Terror which accompanied it. To Kaganovich is attributed the expression 'Why wail over broken eggs when we are trying to make an omelette'. By such a man was the Moscow Metro built.

BUILDING THE METRO
From Siberian mines to the Moscow Metro

About 30,000 Russian labourers worked on the first line, the *Sokolnicheskaya*, an 8 km (4.9 mile) line running from *Sokolniki* in the North East to *Park Kultury* in the South West. Labourers were drawn from the coal mines of Siberia and the Ukraine, construction workers from the steelworks of Magnitogorsk and from the Siberian railway. Before beginning work engineers from Moscow had visited London, the home of the world's oldest underground railway, to learn what they could about building and running such a system. Much of the early design and construction work was carried out under the supervision of British engineers. A tunnelling shield was built in Britain and imported to Moscow, (no doubt paid for with the proceeds of the Ukrainian famine) the design later being copied and reproduced in shields made in Russia. The removal of the soil excavated to make the tunnels was executed by labourers with wheelbarrows from which it was dumped in adjoining streets. Further removal to points outside the city was impeded by the terrible Russian winters which froze the dumps solid.

For frozen soil

The NKVD steps in

Based upon British experience, escalators rather than lifts were incorporated in the station designs from the start and the electrical power system and rolling stock also drew upon London's experience. Once the Soviet authorities felt that they had learned all they needed to know the British engineers, employees of Metropolitan Vickers, were arrested by the NKVD (predecessors of the KGB), tried on charges of espionage and deported. It seems that Stalin and the even more paranoid Lavrenti Beria, the infamous head of the NKVD, feared that the British engineers were learning too much about the layout of the Russian capital.

A TRIUMPH OF SOCIALISM
Song of the Joyous Metro

This first line was opened on 15 May 1935. Almost 300,000 Muscovites used the line in its early days and it was celebrated as a triumph of Socialist enterprise in the service of citizens, with extravagant claims about its superiority to other (capitalist) systems. A 'Song of the Joyous Metro' was written for the opening and performed at the Bolshoi theatre. Much was made of the fact that its trains could travel at 80 kmph (49.7 mph), faster than the capitalist systems of London, New York and Paris. Shortly afterwards a group of engineers from the London Underground were invited to visit and admire this latest triumph of Socialism and Frank Pick, the Chief Executive of London Transport, was awarded an Honorary badge of merit by Stalin, surely a unique distinction for a man who was such a senior officer of what was then still a private company.

STATION MONUMENTS TO SOCIALIST REALISM: AND GANTS HILL
Art should serve politics

No expense was spared in the design and decoration of the early stations. A common feature is a vaulted central hall running the length of the stations, with short passages leading to the less ornate platforms on either side. The station at Gants Hill on the Central Line in Essex, built in the 1930s, follows a similar pattern, in tribute to the Moscow designs which were being prepared in consultation with the London Underground engineers at the time before their arrest by the NKVD. It is certainly an impressive structure for a modest suburban station and won an award for architectural merit at the Festival of Britain in 1951. Every opportunity was taken by Kaganovich and Khrushchev to portray the virtues of triumphant socialism in station designs, using the style which became known as Socialist Realism, a creed which reflected the theories of Lenin's mentor Nikolay Chernyshevsky, that 'art should serve politics'. Generous use was made of reflective marble, murals, extravagant lighting including chandeliers, and stained glass. Just as the mediaeval cathedrals of Europe celebrated the heroes and martyrs of Christianity, the murals of the Moscow Metro were designed to reflect *svetloe budushchee* (a radiant future) featuring panels showing daily life of Soviet citizens in the Socialist state: muscular workers brandishing hammers and sickles; rosy-cheeked women on collective farms with sheaves of wheat; heroes of productive labour; and exemplars of sporting prowess. During World War II, the station designs reflected the triumphs of the Soviet armed forces.

EXTRAORDINARY FACT

In the years that followed, the network was steadily expanded in accordance with the plan, each line running across the city and being allocated a number and a colour. Eventually thirteen radial lines and two Circles featured in the network by 2020, with others planned. As new designs of rolling stock were introduced each was given a new Alpha-numeric designation. The work continued throughout World War II and during the siege of Moscow in 1941–2 the platforms were used as shelters from the Nazi forces and the offices of the Council of Ministers were moved to the magnificent Mayakovskaya station on the Zamoskvoretskaya line, which had been completed in 1938. On several occasions Stalin's speeches were recorded and filmed in this unlikely location. During this period the Metro had one narrow escape. In October 1941, with Nazi forces within 64 km (40 miles) of Moscow, Kaganovich received an order to close the Metro and to prepare proposals for its destruction. On 16 October 1941, at the height of the panic, as plans were being made to move the government out of Moscow, the Metro was closed – the only day in its history that it carried no passengers. That same evening the order to prepare to destroy the network was cancelled. Stalin and the government remained in the capital and the Metro survived.

EXTRAORDINARY FACT

Nuclear shelters

In the post-Stalin period – as the network expanded with the construction of further lines – Nikita Khrushchev, both as a break with the Stalinism which he denounced and as an economic measure, decreed

that more modest designs should be adopted and these lines, built in the 1950s, were also designed to withstand a nuclear attack. Park Pobedy station, for example, is 74 metres (242.7 feet) beneath the surface. By comparison Hampstead, the deepest station on the London Underground, is 58 metres (190.2 feet) beneath Hampstead Heath. Yet the original lines, opened between 1935 and 1950, are still regarded as fine examples of Soviet Socialist design and many of these early stations are tourist destinations in their own right. The 80th anniversary of the Metro in 2015 was celebrated by a procession of renovated trains, some dating from the 1930s, passing round the magnificent stations of Moscow's Circle Line to the accompaniment of brass bands while actors, dressed in costumes of the 1930s, played the parts of passengers of the period.

Socialist women welcome

From the earliest days, but especially during the war when men were required for the Red Army, women have been very well represented amongst the Metro staff and have been employed in many roles including drivers. A female voice announces the arrival of outbound trains (anti-clockwise on the Circles) and a male voice announces inbound and clockwise arrivals. The system has always offered very cheap fares. Until the 1990s there was a flat fare of five kopeks (a few pence) and the fare at present is about 80 pence. Students can buy a year's travel for less than £5. This encourages citizens to use the Metro rather than Moscow's congested and fume-laden streets.

QUICK FACTS

TERRORIST ATTACKS The Metro has sometimes been a target for terrorists. In January 1977 a bomb went off in a crowded train, killing seven and injuring many more. Three people of Armenian descent were executed. Two incidents in 2004 which resulted in the deaths of over fifty were blamed on Islamic Chechen terrorists and in 2010 two bombs on the original Sokolnicheskaya line, one at the Lubyanka station, near the former headquarters of the KGB, and another at the Park Kultury station, killed over fifty people. An Islamic group based in the Caucasus claimed responsibility.

The Mystery of Metro 2 or D6

There are persistent rumours, from multiple sources of widely varying authenticity, of a shadow Metro for use by Stalin, the FSB (successors to the KGB) or the Russian government in the event of nuclear war. It was allegedly codenamed D6 by the KGB and is more commonly referred to as Metro 2. When a former head of the Moscow Metro was questioned about this supposed separate system, he replied that he would be surprised if it did not exist. Given the paranoid nature of the Soviet government and its successors it is only to be expected that some such facility exists in Moscow.

'A HUGE UNDERGROUND CITY'
Beware of assassins

The Soviet defector Oleg Gordievsky – who worked for British Intelligence for eleven years before being smuggled out of Russia in 1985 in circumstances that would do justice to James Bond – confirmed that a 'huge underground city' did indeed exist with its own communications network. A former adviser to Mikhail Gorbachev and Boris Yeltsin reported that in Stalin's era a single track underground line was constructed to link the Kremlin and Stalin's own Dacha on the outskirts of Moscow to accommodate Stalin's paranoia about assassins but that it was no longer in use in 2004. In 1991 the US Department of Defence reported the existence of a more elaborate system of subways linking the Kremlin and other key facilities with an underground bunker capable of accommodating 10,000 people in the vicinity of Moscow State

University, about 5 km (3 miles) to the South West of Moscow.
A photograph of a ventilation shaft near the university suggests
the existence of a subterranean structure. Other reports have
four lines connecting the Kremlin with the headquarters
of the FSB, a VIP terminal at Vnukovo airport beyond the
university and with an underground town at Ramenki further
to the south-west. Other reports claimed that there was
accommodation for 30,000 people, supposedly built in the
1960s and 1970s at the height of the Cold War.

A MYSTERIOUS DEATH
'They will not show you'

A further scenario was presented by Igor Malashenko,
founder of an independent TV station, who in 1992
told America's *Time* magazine of a bunker in the north-east
of Moscow which was flooded and unusable, a fate which he
also ascribed to the facilities to the south-west at Moscow
State University. Independent TV stations have not been
popular with the authorities during the Putin era and in 2009
Malashenko left Russia to live in Spain, dying mysteriously in
February 2019. In 1992, early in the post-Soviet era, accounts
of *Metro 2* appeared in magazines, one claiming to have
identified secret bunkers served by an underground railway
which were equipped with spacious accommodation intended
for the leadership of the Politburo and their families. The
Soviet leader Leonid Brezhnev had supposedly once visited
one of the bunkers and presented the head of the KGB Yuri
Andropov (Brezhnev's successor) with an award. A leader of
a Moscow Metro trade union informed a Russian magazine
that some years previously drivers had been interviewed

to work on a secret underground railway facility driving a battery–powered locomotive and one passenger car: clearly not a mass transit facility! I think we may assume that some such facility exists, probably served by an electric railway but, in the words of Oleg Gordievski, still living in hiding in England and perhaps the most reliable authority 'They will not show you. They will never of course'.

Lines of Moscow Metro

	Line name, number, colour	First opened	Latest extension	Length (km)	Stations
1	Sokolnicheskaya	1935	2019	44.5	26
2	Zamoskvoretskaya	1938	2018	42.8	24
3	Arbatsko-Pokrovskaya	1938	2012	45.1	22
4	Filyovskaya	1958 (1935)	2006	14.9	13
5	Koltsevaya (Circle)	1950	1954	19.3	12
6	Kaluzhsko-Rizhskaya	1958	1990	37.8	24
7	Tagansko-Krasnopresnenskaya	1966	2015	42.2	23
8	Kalininskaya[Note 2]	1979	2012	16.3	8
8A	Solntsevskaya[Note 2]	2014	2018	24.8	12
9	Serpukhovsko-Timiryazevskaya	1983	2002	41.5	25
10	Lyublinsko-Dmitrovskaya	1995	2018	38.3	23
11	Bolshaya Koltsevaya (Big Circle)	2018	2018	12.6	6
12	Butovskaya	2003	2014	10.0	7
14	Moscow Central Circle	2016	2016	54.0	31
15	Nekrasovskaya	2019	2020	22.3	10
				462.1	**264**

Line 13 is a Monorail 4.7 km long and is omitted from this list

The New York Subway

FIRST IN AMERICA

The New York Subway entered service in October 1904, the first in the American continent though, as we shall see, an early attempt to create an underground railroad for what is still the most populous city in the USA had been made more than thirty years earlier. The subway has 472 stations, more than any other system, served 24 hours a day, and is one of the most intensively used subways in the world, with 394 km (244.8 miles) of routes. It operates on 600–650 volts DC drawing power from a third rail. On its first day it carried over 150,000 passengers who each paid 5 cents, while in its first full year of operation, 1905, it carried 448 million passengers. About 40 per cent of the system is above ground and on 23 September 2014, it carried a record 6.1 million passengers. It now carries 1.7 billion passengers a year, all but three of the routes passing beneath Manhattan Island.

FIVE BOROUGHS
= *One city*

M anhattan is the home of Wall Street and the financial district, Broadway with its theatres, Central Park and Harlem but there is more to New York City than Manhattan. The other routes serve three of the other boroughs that together constitute the city – Brooklyn and Queens on Long

Island and the Bronx on the mainland. The fifth borough, Staten Island (also known as Richmond) has a separate rail service.

Like the London system, in its early days it consisted of a number of separate organizations but by 1940 the two private companies were bought out by the City and they are now all managed by the New York City Transit Authority (NYTA). At the same time other transport services including buses and elevated railroads passed into the ownership of the City,

Five boroughs of New York

leaving it with debts which, over the following decades, have meant that maintaining and upgrading the facilities has often been neglected. A distinction is drawn between *lines* and *routes*. The 'lines' are the physical tracks, the permanent way. The 'routes', or 'services' are the trains that run over them and the distinction simply reflects the fact that some services share the same track in parts – as in London where, for example, three services, the Metropolitan, Hammersmith & City and Circle Lines share the same track and platforms running through such stations as King's Cross St Pancras.

EXPRESS AND STOPPING SERVICES
Thinking ahead

The subway engineers designing the New York system had visited London to examine its underground railway which had been running for almost 40 years. The New York delegation, with commendable foresight, envisaged the expansion of the Manhattan lines into the outer boroughs and even to New Jersey across the Hudson river, so the New York subway has, from the early days, run both express services for longer distance travellers stopping at a few busy stations; and stopping services calling at every station, an arrangement which required twice as many tracks as were needed by systems such as London's whose trains call at every station. Each route has its own letter or number displayed on the front of the train and each line has its own name and colour, as in London. The best way to understand the system is by consulting the official subway map originally designed in 1979 by the company of Michael Hertz (1932−2020). The lines and routes are as follows:

Train Services	Line Name	Express	Local
1 **2** **3**	Broadway − 7th Ave.	**2** **3**	**1**
4 **5** **6** **◆6**	Lexington Ave.	**4** **5** **◆6**	**6**
7 **◆7**	Flushing	**◆7**	**7**
A **C** **E**	8th Ave.	**A**	**C** **E**
B **D** **F** **M**	6th Ave.	**B** **D**	**F** **M**
N **Q** **R** **W**	Broadway	**N** **Q**	**R** **W**
J **Z**	Nassau St.	**J** **Z**	
L	Canarsie		**L**
G	Crosstown		**G**
S	Various shuttles*		

There are six shuttles; 42nd Street, Rockaway Park and Franklin Avenue run all day. Dyre Avenue, Lefferts Boulevard and Myrtle Avenue are late night shuttles.

DID YOU KNOW?

Early failure: pneumatic propulsion

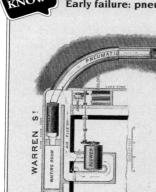

Beach pneumatic plan

The first attempt to create an underground system for New York was made by Alfred Ely Beach (1826–96), a wealthy publisher and inventor who designed a tunnelling shield based upon the original shield of Marc Brunel (see TBMs) though Beach's shield was circular in shape. He had also been inspired by the Metropolitan Railway in London (see *The Metropolitan Railway*) which had been opened in 1863 to deal with the appalling traffic congestion in London, a problem which was, by 1860, beginning to afflict New York. Such was the road traffic that by the 1860s it was becoming common for citizens to complain about the hazards and delays involved in crossing the avenues. With his shield Beach bored a tunnel about 95 metres (311 feet) in length beneath Broadway. The trains were to be drawn along by a system of pneumatic propulsion, a vacuum in a tube laid between the rails drawing the train along the rails. This idea was tried earlier, and abandoned, by Isambard Kingdom Brunel on a track which still carries trains south from Exeter towards Torquay in Devon, England. The Beach Pneumatic Transit was no more successful as a means of locomotion than Brunel's had been and was abandoned, the tunnel's remnants now lying beneath City Hall.

RAILWAYS IN THE AIR
'New York, unlike London, does not suffer from fogs'

The streets of Manhattan are designed to a grid pattern by which the avenues, such as Fifth Avenue and Madison Avenue run the length of Manhattan Island and the streets run across the avenues. Broadway runs diagonally across the streets and avenues. The long, straight avenues lent themselves to the construction of a series of elevated railroads running along them, drawn by steam engines. The first entered service in 1868, initially drawn by cables and by 1897 a substantial network of such elevated lines existed over 2nd, 3rd 6th and 9th Avenues, the trains running at about 16 kmph (10 mph) and dependent upon the alertness of the drivers to avoid collisions since there were no signals. A visiting Englishman observed that it was 'fortunate that New York, unlike London, does not suffer from fogs'! But the smoke made by the steam engines and the noise made by metal wheels on metal rails in close proximity to homes, factories and offices was becoming intolerable. Moreover New York is subject to fierce blizzards to which the elevated railroads were vulnerable, a particularly bad one in 1888 bringing the city to a standstill.

1855 map of New York City

EXTRAORDINARY FACT

Still available for car chases

A proposal for the construction of an underground railroad was accepted in 1894 and on 24 March 1901, Mayor Robert Van Wyck, the first person to assume the office of mayor for all five boroughs, dug the first spadeful of earth for what was to become the first stage in New York's Underground Railroad. It was built in haste which meant that the residents whose homes bordered the route of the line were kept awake at night by the incessant noise until an embargo was imposed on working after 11.00 pm. The line opened to passengers on 27 October 1904, running 15 km (9.3 miles) from City Hall to 145th Street in Harlem, much of it built beneath Broadway and known at the time as the Manhattan Main Line and later as the Broadway Line. In the years that followed the network expanded rapidly, reaching over 300 km (186.4 miles) by 1920. The elevated railroads gradually closed in Manhattan though they may still be seen in the outlying boroughs, a fragment still surviving in Manhattan itself in the vicinity of 125th Street and Broadway. The streets beneath the surviving elevated railroads have been used for the filming of car chases by Hollywood studios.

MANHATTAN SCHIST
Picks, shovels and explosives

The underlying geology of New York, especially Manhattan, where the subway began and is at its densest, is of very hard rock, a good foundation for the skyscrapers for which New York became famous the following century. Near the surface is soil and gravel of the kind disturbed by the spade of mayor Van Wyck but the underlying bedrock is *Manhattan Schist*, a sedimentary rock which resists picks, shovels and tunnelling machinery much more firmly than soil and gravel or London Clay. In midtown Manhattan, where many skyscrapers are found, the bedrock is close to the surface and it is actually visible in parts of Central Park. Most of the tracks for the first line were built by the cut and cover method employed for the early lines in London. In some cases the excavation had to be carried out without disturbing the flow of traffic on the congested avenues which the early lines followed. This was done by digging a trench on either side of the avenue and then excavating a tunnel from the trench on one side to the trench on the other, just beneath the surface. From these transverse trenches the train tunnels were then driven in either direction beneath the avenues to create the space for the tracks and the stations.

Most of the work was carried out manually by almost 8,000 immigrant workers, using picks and shovels, though tunnel boring machines were used for later lines. Explosive charges were used when necessary to deal with bedrock, while the soil and gravel were vulnerable to flooding both by rain and by ingress from the East and Hudson Rivers. These lie on either side of the narrow strip of land which constitutes Manhattan Island. This required the use of pumps which remain a feature of the network. Coffer dams were used to cross rivers such as the Harlem river which separates Manhattan from the Bronx. These were used to seal off sections of a river from which water was pumped, leaving a dry bed across which tubes could be laid to carry the tracks. Where the bedrock was encountered, mechanical drills were sometimes used.

Ropeways

The spoil was removed by ropeways running above the trenches. Spoil was loaded into hoppers hanging from the ropeways which, powered by electricity, carried them to offloading points where the spoil was emptied into carts which bore it away. The width of the avenues enabled four tracks to be built, permitting stopping trains and expresses to run in each direction. Some lines have three tracks, the third being reversible to carry passengers into the city in the morning peak and out in the evenings. Most of the stations, being near the surface, were reached by staircases rather than elevators. The construction was made more difficult by the need to displace sewers, water pipes and other utilities as well as avoiding damage to the foundations of the tall buildings which were already springing up in parts of Manhattan and those of the elevated railroads, many of which did not long survive the arrival of the subways.

QUICK FACTS

FARES Many stations in Manhattan have mezzanine floors where the passenger can pay a fare which is registered on a Metrocard, introduced in 1993 and from which the passenger can access all platforms, thus freeing passengers from the need to cross the congested streets to reach the platform required. Since most of the early stations are sub-surface rather than deep tubes, escalators and elevators were often not installed and many stations have been modified by the addition of such facilities since the *Americans with Disabilities Act* took effect in 1990. The platforms are up to 180 metres (590 feet) long to accommodate 8 car stopping or 11 car express trains. The flat fare is $2.75 (about £1.96) with concessions for senior and disabled citizens and the Metrocard may also be used on buses. It is gradually being superseded by a contactless system using debit or credit cards but will remain in use for some years.

NEW SIGNALLING FOR MORE TRAINS
Lock and Block

The use of the subway by New Yorkers has often pressed against the limits of its capacity. In April 2013 *New York Magazine* claimed that it was more crowded than it had been since the 1940s, with daily usage regularly exceeding 6 million passengers. Two of the Express lines, the IRT Lexington Avenue Line and the IND Queens Boulevard Line were particularly overcrowded during the morning and evening peaks, leading to delays while passengers struggled to board already crowded trains. Attempts to relieve the congestion have often relied upon improved methods of signalling to enable more trains to run safely on the same track. Since the 19th century railroad signalling has depended upon a 'lock and block' system in which the track has been divided into sections, only one train being allowed into each section at any one time. Each section, or 'block' is about 300 metres (984.2 feet) long on the subway and entry to the section is controlled by a signal, a red signal in effect 'locking out' a following train from a section already occupied. This is known as a 'fixed block' system. The signalling for the early days of the New York subway was designed by an engineer called George Gibbs who for the first time introduced a device which would alert a driver if he passed a red signal – an arm projecting from the signal gantry which would activate the brakes on the train. To overcome the problems of congestion a new signalling system has been introduced on some lines called Communications Based Train Control (CBTC). This depends upon radio communications between the train, the track and a central controller so that the exact position and speed of each train is known. The train is in effect its own block consisting of the train itself and a 'trail' behind it which no other train can enter. It is known as a 'moving block' system and enables more trains to run simultaneously on a given length of track. It was first tested on the Canarsie route because it doesn't share its track with any other service. The CBTC system enabled the number of trains per hour to increase from 15 to 26. It has since been extended to other lines and it is anticipated that it will cost up to $15 billion (£10.6 billion) to complete the resignallling of the entire system over 15 years. Station platform controllers have also been deployed on several lines to manage the movement of passengers during busy periods.

CRIMINALS AND BROKEN WINDOWS
War on graffiti and Guardian Angels

The subway has long been a haven for criminals and in the 1970s usage of the system began to fall to levels not seen since its early days, fear of crime being one of the principal reasons. In 1975 the city itself came close to bankruptcy and the city's poor financial state was reflected in poor maintenance of the track and rolling stock, a problem made worse by the policy of running 24 hour a day services on all lines. To service the track and signalling, special closures have to be made, usually at weekends, to enable engineers to gain access to replace and upgrade these facilities. By the 1980s there was a serious problem with crime throughout the city and the authorities adopted what became known as the

Broken Windows approach to the problem, based on the belief that low level crime such as broken windows and anti-social behaviour created an environment that led to more serious offences. This was adopted by mayor Rudy Giuliani and his police commissioner William Bratton.

At about the same time the New York City Transit Authority took on the problem of graffiti on subway rolling stock with trains thoroughly cleaned and night patrols making it more difficult for graffiti artists to gain access to the trains. One of the consequences of the level of crime was the foundation of the *Guardian Angels* by Curtis Sliwa with twelve followers. They were unarmed, but they wore distinctive red berets, white T-shirts and red jackets declaring that they were crime fighters who patrolled troubled lines in groups. At first they attracted the hostility of the police but were later recognized as useful in pacifying lawless and gang-ridden parts of the subway. They spread to many other cities (including, briefly, London) and together with other measures helped to bring about a reduction in crime on the network.

Deafening

As the city recovered financially new subway cars were ordered, maintenance improved and passengers returned to reach record levels in the second decade of the 21st century. Noise was also a problem. The Subway operates about 6,500 cars and the noise generated by steel wheels on steel rails was found, by Columbia University's School of Public Health, to generate levels of over 90 decibels in trains and on platforms, rising to 100 decibels in some stations. Prolonged exposure to such levels may lead to hearing loss for staff or passengers. Steps to reduce the noise include the use of sound absorption materials on track and on station ceilings.

QUICK FACTS

• **SUICIDE** Suicides on the subway have led the Subway management to consider the installation of platform edge doors in central areas of the kind found on the Jubilee Line in London. The attacks of 9/11 severely disrupted the lines in the vicinity of the World Trade Centre. In 2009 a group of Islamist extremists pleaded guilty to plotting suicide bombings on the system and for a while it was forbidden to take photographs of the Subway.

HURRICANES, BLIZZARDS AND RATS
Track maintenance and the future

Extreme weather events associated with the phenomenon of global warming are a recurrent problem. Even on a dry day more than ten million gallons of water are pumped out of the system. On 8 August 2007, after a heavy summer storm, much of the system flooded, disabling the signalling and obliging the current to be cut off. In August 2011 the service suffered the first ever suspension of service caused by weather when the subway was closed at midday in anticipation of Hurricane Irene. In October 2012 Hurricane Sandy caused most of the system to be shut down as nine tunnels were flooded. It was several days before a reasonable level of service was restored. And in 2015 Andrew Cuomo, governor of New York State, ordered the closure of the system as a blizzard approached, threatening up to 75 cm (29 in) of snow.

Some stations in the central area are ridden with vermin attracted by rubbish discarded by passengers and rats have been known to bite passengers. The rubbish also causes track fires and the vacuum trains (like London's 'big yellow duster') have long suffered from poor maintenance. In 2016 a study of the metro systems in the USA found that the New York Subway was the dirtiest of all. New vacuum trains were ordered and an operation called 'Track Sweep' was announced. In June 2017 Governor Andrew Cuomo declared a state of emergency for the City after a series of accidents – including derailments and track fires – and shortly afterwards a $9 billion (£6.3 billion) investment plan was launched to improve to upgrade maintenance, safety and cleanliness.

The Paris Métro

The Paris Métro, or *Métropolitain de Paris*, is the busiest underground railway system in Western Europe. It has sixteen lines, with four more under construction, 302 stations and 214 km of track of which 197 km (122.4 miles) are underground. It carries 1.5 billion passengers a year with a daily total of over 4 million. Some lines are elevated, including some which cross the river Seine. The number of cars in each train varies from three to eight, dependent upon the line, with most trains having five cars. Since 1949 it has been managed by the *Régie Autonome des Transports Parisiens* (RATP) a state-owned body. A flat fare of €1.90 (£1.64) is charged for a single journey but books of ten tickets can be bought for €16.90 (£14.60) at Métro stations, tourist offices and on Eurostar trains. The City is also served by the *Réseau Express Régional* which is jointly managed by the RATP and the SNCF. The Métro lines are as follows and it can be seen that such is the density of the system within Paris that the distance between stations, on average 548 metres (1,797.9 feet), is less than in most other systems, the intention being that within central Paris no-one should have to walk more than 500 metres (1,640.4 feet) to a Métro station. In 2014 Anne Hidalgo was elected and announced a new transport system, Le Grand Paris Express, including four new Métro lines with 68 stations and 200 kms (124.2 miles) of track.

Line		Opened	Stations served	Length	Average distance between stations	Journeys made (2017)	Termini
1	Line 1	1900	25	16.6 km	692 m	181.2 million	La Défense Château de Vincennes
2	Line 2	1900	25	12.3 km	513 m	105.2 million	Porte Dauphine Nation
3	Line 3	1904	25	11.7 km	488 m	101.4 million	Pont de Levallois – Bécon Gallieni
3bis	Line 3bis	1971	4	1.3 km	433 m		Porte des Lilas Gambetta
4	Line 4	1908	27	12.1 km	438 m	155.9 million	Porte de Clignancourt Mairie de Montrouge
5	Line 5	1906	22	14.6 km	697 m	110.9 million	Bobigny – Pablo Picasso Place d'Italie
6	Line 6	1909	28	13.6 km	504 m	114.3 million	Charles de Gaulle– Étoile Nation
7	Line 7	1910	38	22.4 km	605 m	135.1 million	La Courneuve – 8 mai 1945 Villejuif – Louis Aragon Mairie d'Ivry
7bis	Line 7bis	1967	8	3.1 km	443 m		Louis Blanc Pré-Saint-Gervais
8	Line 8	1913	38	23.4 km	614 m	105.5 million	Balard Pointe du Lac
9	Line 9	1922	37	19.6 km	544 m	137.9 million	Pont de Sèvres Mairie de Montreuil
10	Line 10	1923	23	11.7 km	532 m	45.3 million	Boulogne – Pont de Saint-Cloud Gare d'Austerlitz
11	Line 11	1935	13	6.3 km	525 m	47.1 million	Châtelet Mairie des Lilas
12	Line 12	1910	29	13.9 km	515 m	84.3 million	Front Populaire Mairie d'Issy
13	Line 13	1911	32	24.3 km	776 m	131.4 million	Châtillon – Montrouge Saint-Denis – Université Les Courtilles
14	Line 14	1998	9	9 km	1,075 m	83.3 million	Saint-Lazare Olympiades

A RIOTOUS POPULATION
No knee breeches!

The Paris Métro owes its origin in some degree to the riotous habits of the Parisian underclass, referred to as the *sans-culottes* (literally 'without knee breeches') who had instigated the storming of the Bastille in 1789. In 1848 a riot against King Louis Philippe (1773–1850) brought Louis Napoleon, nephew of Bonaparte, to the French throne and a further riot four years later (the ninth riot by Parisians since 1825) made him Emperor Napoleon III, with more powers than any French leader since those exercised by his late uncle. Reflecting upon the riotous tendencies of his fellow citizens, the Emperor appointed Georges-Eugene Haussmann as prefect of the Seine, with instructions to tear down the warren of streets in the centre of Paris. These harboured the rioting *sans-culottes* and were easy to barricade so Haussmann replaced them with the broad avenues (one named Boulevard Haussmann) which characterize Paris to this day. The avenues and boulevards were connected to railway termini so that in the event of disturbances cavalry and artillery could be brought into the city and deployed along the avenues to quell the rioters.

QUICK FACTS

WHO'S IN CHARGE? Haussmann (1809–91) was Prefect of the Seine from 1853 to 1870, in all but name mayor of Paris, though the suspicion felt by the government towards the city's unruly inhabitants was such that Paris, alone amongst French cities, was denied a mayor until 1976.

'THE FIRST PROLETARIAN REVOLUTIONARIES'
Karl Marx approves

The need for Haussmann's attempts to subdue the populace was further emphasized in his final year in office when, following France's defeat in the Franco-Prussian War of 1870−1, the inhabitants of Paris, in a final act of defiance, set up the Commune. From March to May 1871 the *Communards* opposed the Government's attempts to reach a peace settlement with the Prussians. Karl Marx called the communards 'The first Proletarian Revolutionaries'. With their headquarters in Montmartre they fought the armies of their own government, executed the Archbishop of Paris and made their last stand in the Père Lachaise cemetery, the episode culminating in *la semaine sanglante* (the bloody week) and an estimated 20,000 deaths − more bloodshed than had occurred during Robespierre's reign of terror following the Revolution of 1789. The victorious government regarded the bloodshed as a final reckoning with the Parisians' revolutionary tendencies and it set a pattern of hostility between national government and capital city that coloured much of what followed. To this day Parisians make an annual pilgrimage to Père Lachaise in memory of the martyrs.

MAIN LINE TRAINS NOT WANTED HERE

In 1871 a team of engineers was invited by Haussmann's successors, the General Council of the Seine, to devise an urban railway system which would meet the needs of the expanding population. Some favoured elevated railways like those following the avenues in New York (see **Raiways in the Air***) while others argued for an underground system. The arguments continued for 20 years and involved such illustrious names as the writers Guy de Maupassant and Victor Hugo and, perhaps speaking with more authority, the engineer Gustave Eiffel.*

The mutual distrust between the government of France and its capital city continued to smoulder. Parisians were resistant to the idea that main line railways should be extended to create a new underground network within the city, a plan favoured by the government. The city commissioned the engineer Jean-Baptiste Berlier, (1841–1911) who had already designed a system of pneumatic tubes for Paris' postal network, to design a rail system which would be protected from interference by the national government.

★ AMAZING FACT ★

KEEP RIGHT

Berlier suggested that the tracks should be 1300 mm (4 ft 2 in) in width, narrower than the standard 1435 mm (4 ft 8.5 in) gauge on which the surface railways ran, to insulate the system against a takeover by the main line railways. As a compromise to end the long-running quarrel the standard gauge was adopted but the tunnels were cut too narrow for surface train rolling stock. Moreover, the Métro trains ran on the right rather than on the left as the main line trains did, a further protection against any incursions from the world beyond!

WATCH YOUR STEP
A hole in the Arc de Triomphe

The main entrance of the Exposition Universelle 1889

The task of designing the system was finally passed to the City Engineer of Paris, Fulgence Bienvenüe (1852−1936). Construction began in 1898 with the aim of opening the line in time for the Paris *Exposition Universelle* (World's Fair) in April 1900. The geology of Paris is quite complex with some clay and some hard rock, while at one point the tunnels had to pass through some disused gypsum quarries which had been used as rubbish dumps. Most of the work was done manually, by picks and shovels and at one point a portion of the Champs-Élysées subsided into the tunnel and had to be boarded off while in the vicinity of the Arc de Triomphe a hole appeared 20 metres (65.6 feet) in length into which two pedestrians fell, fortunately without serious injury. The service between Porte Maillot and Porte de Vincennes starting in July 1900. Other lines soon followed, with six lines operating by 1909, five of them radiating from Place de l'Étoile.

> **QUICK FACTS**
>
> **IS THAT GARLIC I CAN SMELL?** The Métro was well received by the citizens despite some barbed comments in the Baedeker Guide of 1904. Comparing it to the London Underground the guide's verdict was that 'the atmosphere is similarly oppressive to susceptible people' and went on to remark that whereas the prevailing odour on the London tubes was that of sulphur, in Paris it was garlic, which would surely be preferable!

PUT THAT FIRE OUT!
Problem becomes catastrophe

Shortly before the Baedeker guide of 1904 was published the Métro suffered the worst accident in its history to date. A 4-car train reaching the Boulevard Barbes station, on an elevated viaduct near the Gare du Nord, had a small fire burning in the leading coach. The passengers disembarked and, instead of extinguishing the modest blaze, a following 8-car train, whose passengers also disembarked, was brought forward and instructed to propel the burning train to a depot eleven stations along the line. As the train gathered speed the draught in the tunnel fanned the flames and an attempt by the stationmaster at Rue des Couronnes to stop the train and extinguish the blaze was resisted by the train crew. Shortly afterwards, as it approached the station in a deep tunnel at Menilmontant the entire train burst into flames, sending acrid smoke back towards Rue des Couronnes station where a third train, crowded with passengers from the first two, was just arriving. As the station, and the passengers, were enveloped in the fumes the lights failed and many of the choking passengers failed to find the only exit from the station. 84 passengers were suffocated. There was much criticism of the fact that exits and entrances to the system were often few and inconspicuous. Following much public criticism further entrances were installed, together with auxiliary lighting systems.

ART NOUVEAU

A policy of having small and inconspicuous entrances to stations appears to have been due to the sensitivity of Parisians about despoiling Haussmann's magnificent boulevards and squares with ugly commercial buildings. However the stations, notably the entrances, are now regarded as supreme examples of the **Art**

Nouveau *style, which was at the height of its popularity at the time the Métro was built. Its origins may be traced back to William Morris and the Arts and Crafts movement which was founded in reaction to the cheap, mass processed products of the factories of the industrial revolution, but it reached its zenith in France at the turn of the 19th and 20th centuries, being characterized by gentle, sinuous lines and pastel shades.*

Art Nouveau Metro sign

HECTOR GUIMARD
Glass and foliage

The entrances were designed by Hector Guimard (1867–1942), one of the style's most prominent and successful advocates. 80 of Guimard's entrances are still in use. They are characterized by elaborate glass canopies and cast-iron balustrades in sinuous lines resembling foliage topped with orange, globe-shaped lights on iron stems between which is suspended the *Métro* sign. The Art Nouveau style was also carried through into the early stations themselves which typically have two central tracks between two platforms, each about 4 metres (13 feet) wide, the area being vaulted and the walls covered by white tiles. Many of the early stations in the central area have been restored and their distinctive Art Nouveau styling retained, with the originals still in place at the Porte Dauphine and Abbesses stations. Some of the Guimard entrances have been replaced and the originals have been given to adorn the entrances to underground stations in other cities including Lisbon, Mexico City and Chicago.

Metropolitan station — Place de la Bastille

QUICK FACTS

ALL IN A NAME The Métro name was probably inspired by London's Metropolitan Railway. The word itself never caught on in England but thanks to its adoption by its French cousin it has been adopted by most other underground railway systems of the world.

BEYOND THE WALLS

The Parisians' suspicion of their fellow countrymen was such that the early Métro Lines were confined to the area within the City walls, which had been built as fortifications in the 1840s but had proved useless against Prussian artillery. In the 1930s the Métro lines were gradually extended to the inner suburbs, beginning with line 9 to Boulogne–Billancourt. Others soon followed, interrupted by World War II but by 1949 eight lines had been extended in this way. As the population grew rapidly from the 1950s and more commuters arrived at the main line railway termini on the outskirts of the city centre, the Métro became seriously overcrowded and the very short distances between stations meant that journeys were slow as well as uncomfortably congested.

FIVE LINES, 257 STATIONS, 587 KM (364 MILES)
The RER

The RER has five lines, denoted by the letters A to E to avoid confusion with the Métro lines 1 to 14. It is jointly owned by the RATP and the SNCF. Construction of the RER began in 1961. The first new station, *Nation*, was completed in 1969 and the first two lines, A and B, began to operate in 1977 with the remaining three following, the last to date, Line E, entering service in 1999. The RER has 587 km (364.7 miles) of track (against 214 km (132.9 miles) for the Métro) and 257 stations (the Métro has 302). Within the city itself the RER has 76 km (47.2 miles) of dedicated underground tracks and 33 stations, including the nine offering interchanges with the Métro. It carries about 660 million passengers a year, about a third of those who use the Métro, though of course RER passengers travel much longer distances. The RER has much larger tunnels through Paris than the Métro because it draws electric power from overhead catenaries rather than from a third rail as the Métro does and, like the trains of the SNCF, runs on the left while Métro trains run on the right. The large tunnels have enabled double decker trains to be introduced to Line A which, as can be seen from the following table, is the most heavily used.

★ AMAZING FACT ★

THE RER
The solution was to build the *Reseau Express Regional* (RER) an 'express Métro' first conceived in the 1930s and revived by the RATP in the 1950s. It would enable suburban commuter services to travel from distant suburbs directly to the centre of Paris, connecting with Métro services via 9 interchange stations to carry passengers onward to their final destinations when required.

Line name		Opened	Last extension	Stations served	Length	Journeys made (per annum)
A	Line A	1977	1994	46	108.5 km	273 million
B	Line B	1977	1981	47	80.0 km	165 million
C	Line C	1979	2000	84	185.6 km	140 million
D	Line D	1987	1995	59	190.0 km	145 million
E	Line E	1999	2003	22	52.3 km	60 million

EXTRAORDINARY FACT

Stations Cathédrales

The main Métro / RER hub is the station at *Châtelet–Les Halles* with 5 Métro and 3 RER lines. It became the largest underground station on the system and one of the largest in the world. Three other RER stations at *Étoile*, *Nation* and *Auber* were *stations cathedrales*, built deep underground on a much grander scale than other Métro stations and at enormous cost.

*RER C
sur le pont
Rouelle, Paris*

QUICK FACTS

THE IMPRESSIONISTS Line C was created by joining together the suburban lines of two main line stations, Austerlitz and Gare D'Orsay which had the happy and fortuitous outcome of releasing the Gare d'Orsay to become what is possibly the world's finest gallery of impressionist paintings.

Gare D'Orsay

Pneumatic tyres

Since the advent of the RER the Métro has focussed on upgrading rather than extending its facilities. In 1998 Line 14 entered service, the first new line since 1935 and the first with driverless trains. In 2011 driverless operation was introduced on Line 1 with new trains and by 2013 the whole fleet on the line was driverless. Line 4 is at present undergoing conversion to driverless operation which is expected to be completed by 2022. Perhaps the most remarkable innovation has been the introduction of pneumatic tyres on some trains to reduce noise, improve the ride and aid acceleration when the train leaves a station. Inflated with nitrogen as a safeguard against the possibility of fire, they are so designed that if a tyre bursts the steel wheel will simply descend on to the rail. The idea has been exported to a number of systems including those of Hong Kong, Montreal and Tokyo.

The St Petersburg Metro

THE ORDER OF LENIN METRO

On 15 November 1955 the first line of St Petersburg's Metro was opened, with eight stations connecting four of the city's five main railway stations. The line was officially known as the V.I.*Lenin Order of Lenin Leningrad Metropoliten*, a title soon mercifully abbreviated to 'The Leningrad Metro'. Other lines swiftly followed. The system now has five lines with a sixth planned and a total length at present of 125 km (77.6 miles) and 72 stations, carrying 743 million passengers annually. Most of the Rolling stock for St Petersburg, as for most Russian underground systems, is built by a Russian company called *Metrowagonmash* based in the city of Mytishchi north east of Moscow. Some of the trains are built at the Skoda works in the Czech Republic. The trains draw current at 850 volts DC from a third rail.

A CAPITAL BUILT IN A MARSH
Peter the Great

St Petersburg, the former capital of Russia and its second city, with a population of 5.3 million, had to wait until 1955 for its underground railway because of the unique geological challenges posed for its builders. The city owes it origin to Tsar Peter the Great (1682−1725) who, wanting a port which gave an outlet to the west, reclaimed its marshy site from the Baltic Sea and the River Neva in 1703. The

city is, in effect, a series of islands separated by rivers which
from the earliest days impeded movement around the city.
St Petersburg remains the cultural capital of Russia, with the
Winter Palace of the former Tsars, the Hermitage Museum
and the Mariinsky theatre, home of the Mariinsky (former
Kirov) Ballet. It is also a major rail centre with lines to
Finland, Murmansk, Warsaw and Moscow. In 1820 a citizen
submitted a plan to Tsar Alexander I (1777–1825) to build a
tunnel linking the city centre to Vasilyevsky Island, a proposal
which drew forth the withering scorn of the Tsar and an
order to refrain from proposing such foolish schemes in the
future. In 1914, following the outbreak of World War I, the
name was changed from the Germanic *St Petersburg* to the
Russian *Petrograd* and in 1924, following the death of Lenin
it was changed again to *Leningrad* to mark the fact that Lenin
had arrived at the Finland station of the city in 1917 to launch
the Bolshevik revolution. Following the collapse of the Soviet
Union the city reverted to its original name in 1991.

NUCLEAR SHELTERS
86 metres beneath the surface

A s with Moscow, the idea of building tunnels beneath the
city was long resisted by property owners and Russian
Orthodox clergy who feared that such works would damage
the fragile foundations of buildings in the marshy ground. From
1901 there followed a series of proposals to build a railway
system that would be partly elevated above the congested streets
and partly underground to link the city's main railway stations.
There was briefly a proposal to build an elevated station in the
city's magnificent Nevsky Prospekt but it was not until 1938

that the chairman of the city's Soviet appointed an engineer
called Ivan Zubkov as director of the project. At that time
(1924–91) the city was known as Leningrad. The chairman of
the Soviet was Alexei Kosygin (1904–80) who, with Leonid
Brezhnev, toppled Nikita Khrushchev in a coup in 1964. By
April 1941, under Zubkov's direction, over 30 shafts for the
construction work had been sunk across the city. The city
suffered during World War II from a siege by Nazi forces lasting
from September 1941 to January 1944, during which all work
ceased on the Metro. Yet in 1947 the project was revived and
the problem of geology was solved by building the network
beneath the marshy ground at a much greater depth than would
be normal practice. Admiralteyskaya, the deepest station, is 86
metres (282.1 feet) below ground. By comparison the deepest
station on the London Underground is Hampstead, at 58 metres
(190.2 feet) beneath Hampstead Heath. The stations, like those
of Moscow, were also intended to be used as nuclear shelters in
the event of attack.

St Petersburg Metro Lines

Line no. & colour	Full name	Opened	Most recent station opened	Length (km)	Number of stations
(M)1	Kirovsko-Vyborgskaya	15 Nov 1955	29 Dec 1978	29.7	19
(M)2	Moskovsko-Petrogradskaya	29 Apr 1961	22 Dec 2006	30.1	18
(M)3	Nevsko-Vasileostrovskaya	3 Nov 1967	26 May 2018	27.6	12
(M)4	Pravoberezhnaya	30 Dec 1985	7 Mar 2009	11.2	8
(M)5	Frunzensko-Primorskaya	20 Dec 2008	3 Oct 2019	26.2	15
Total:				124.8	72

Magnificent stations

Despite their possible use for the grim purpose of protection against nuclear weapons, the St Petersburg Metro, like those of the early Moscow Metro lines, are regarded as particularly fine examples of modern design, especially the stations at Avtovo and Narvskaya and the early stations have conspicuous and grand entrances on the surface. The later lines, conceived and built after Nikita Khrushchev took power in 1953 following Stalin's death, have less ornamental entrances on the surface but are nevertheless regarded as fine examples of late 20th century design. Some are built to a design known as *horizontal lift*, incorporating a large central hall running the length of the station with platform doors opening on to the trains as they arrive, making the hall where passengers wait much quieter and safer than open platforms. Avtovo station, opened in 1955, is a particularly fine example of the style.

Avtovo station

The Pyongyang Metro

THE LAND OF MYSTERY

The 'Democratic People's Republic of (North) Korea' is the surely world's most enigmatic state. It was founded in 1948 by the Communist leader Kim il Sung who, after his death in 1994, was declared to be 'Eternal President' during the rule of his son, Kim Jong Il and evidently remains so during that of his grandson, Kim Jong Un. Reliable facts about this strange and secretive land are hard to come by and this reservation applies to its capital city, Pyongyang and to its Metro.

WINGED HORSE AND GHOST STATION

Glory, Triumph and Bright Light

Pyongyang is estimated to have a population of about 3 million and is situated on the Taedong River. Construction of its Metro began in 1965 and it consists of two lines, both laid to the standard gauge of 1435 mm (4 ft 8.5 in). One line is called Chollima, named after a winged horse from Korean mythology and runs for about 12 km (7.4 miles) the second is called Hyoksin which means 'renewal' and its tracks are about 10 km (6.2 miles) in length. Between them they have 16 stations and both link the capital's main line railway stations with an interchange station called Chonu where the two lines meet. The stations have names with meanings like 'Glory' and

Chollima

'Triumph' from the nation's revolutionary history rather than geographical features. One station, Kwangmyong ('Bright Light') on the Hyoksin line, has been effectively abandoned since 1995 on account of the fact that it is the site of the Eternal President's mausoleum. Trains pass through the station without stopping.

Kim il Sung (1912–94) took power from the Japanese occupiers at the end of World War II in 1945. In 1950, with the backing of China, he invaded South Korea in a war which lasted for three years. His birthday, 15 April, 'the day of the sun' is the most important holiday in North Korea which has adopted a calendar which dates everything from 1912, the year of the Eternal President's birth.

NO ADVERTISING
THE ETERNAL PRESIDENT

A plan to cross beneath the river Taedong was abandoned when about 100 workers died in an accident building the tunnel so the entire system is confined to the west side of the river. It was designed and built with technical aid from China, who also supplied the first trains, drawing 825 volts from a third rail but since 1997 these have been replaced by rolling stock bought second-hand from the Berlin U-Bahn which runs on 750 volts. Before entering service the advertisements were removed from the Berlin trains and replaced by posters featuring the Eternal President and his son, Kim Jong Il.

EATING FORBIDDEN, READING ENCOURAGED
Trainspotter President

Like much else about North Korea the usage of the system is something of a mystery with estimates varying from 98,600 passengers per day to 700,000, paying a flat fare of 5 North Korean Won, the equivalent of less than half a penny. Tourists are allowed to use the system in tightly guided groups. Smoking and eating in the stations and trains is forbidden and punished with a fine but to cheer up the passengers the official newspaper, the 'Rodong Sinmun', ('Workers' Newspaper') is displayed at each station together with murals and statues extolling the virtues and achievements of socialist workers under the direction of the eternal president and his successors. The stations also play state radio broadcasts which further reinforce these uplifting messages.

★ AMAZING FACT ★

It is not clear why a station was chosen as a site for the mausoleum but a clue may lie an exhibit in the Pyongyang Metro's own museum. It records the fact that during the construction of the Metro the Eternal President was in the habit of visiting the site and offering 'On the spot guidance' to the workforce. This must have been a great comfort to them. Perhaps the eternal leader was a trainspotter?

A SECRET NETWORK?

WHY SO MANY TRAINS?

The entire system lies underground and, like much of the Moscow Metro, on which its designs were based, it was built at a great depth beneath the surface. At a depth of over 100 metres (328 feet) in places the stations can serve as bomb shelters and are fitted with steel blast doors in its access passages to that end. And as in Moscow it is also reported that there is an auxiliary system for use by the government in emergencies and even an underground parade ground on which to assemble troops. This belief derives some credibility from the fact that the government bought from Berlin far more trains than the Metro needs or uses, opening the possibility that they are used on the secret network.

EXTRAORDINARY FACT

A long way down for the air conditioning

It takes about three and a half minutes to reach the platforms from the surface, using escalators from China which may help to explain why the system is not as heavily used as other networks. The depth of the tunnels is such that the temperature remains at a comfortable 18°C (64.4°F) throughout the year in a country noted for very cold winters arriving from Siberia and hot summers. From time to time press reports and satellite images suggest that additional stations are being built but like most other things concerning the land of the eternal president nothing is quite certain.

The Shanghai Metro

THE WORLD'S LARGEST CITY

With its population of over 24 million, 3 million more than the capital Beijing, Shanghai is the most populous city in China and indeed in the world. Its position on the estuary of China's greatest river, where the Yangtse reaches the East China Sea, also gives it a place as China's leading trading and financial centre which explains why it occupies a sensitive place in China's sometimes troubled relationship with the rest of the world.

WORLD'S BUSIEST?
13.2 million passengers in a day

Construction of the city's underground railway, known as the Shanghai Metro, began with Deng's support in 1986, ten years after Mao's death, entering service in May 1993 with the opening of 4.4 km (2.7 miles) Line 1. The network expanded rapidly and now has 16 lines, 676 km (420 miles) of track and 414 stations, against Beijing's 405. It vies with Beijing for the title of the most heavily used system with daily passenger numbers exceeding 10 million on workdays, a record of 13.2 million passengers on 8th March 2019 and annual ridership, like that of Beijing, touching 3.9 billion. By 2025 it is planned that there will be 25 lines with 676 km (420 miles) of track, exceeding that of Peking as it is. Early rolling stock was bought from German companies but later models have been supplied by the Chinese company

Changchun, founded in 1954. The track is laid to the standard gauge of 1435 mm (4 ft 8.5 in) with power drawn at 1500 v DC from catenaries though two lines draw it from a third rail. Fares vary with distance travelled, a journey of 6 km (3.7 miles) costing 3 yuan, about 30 pence, with an extra yuan for each further 10 km (6.2 miles). The city's cosmopolitan character is reflected in the practice of presenting station announcements, ticket machines and visual displays in Mandarin and English.

*Line 1
ticket in use
1995–1997*

EXTRAORDINARY FACT

The Cultural Revolution

In 1949, when Mao Tse-tung proclaimed the foundation of the People's Republic of China, trade was allowed only with other Socialist states and this, together with the mayhem of Mao's 'Cultural Revolution' which followed, led to a decline in Shanghai's fortunes. Following the death of Mao in 1976 and the accession to power of the more pragmatic Deng Xiaoping the city's fortunes revived and it swiftly reclaimed its place as one of the foremost trading and financial centres of the world, alongside Tokyo, London and New York. It is also the world's busiest container port.

Opium Wars

In the mid-19th century, following the Opium Wars, China was obliged by military force to submit to what are still referred to as the 'Unequal treaties' with Western powers, notably Great Britain, France and the United States. The treaties granted concessions to these powers in some of the most prosperous parts of Shanghai within which European and American traders enjoyed a degree of independence from Chinese authority, giving them an advantage over the Chinese themselves. To this day one of the city's wealthiest areas is still referred to as 'The French Concession'. Shanghai became the leading trading and financial centre in Asia, with its famous waterfront the 'Bund' becoming one of the most wealthy and cosmopolitan streets in the world.

Shanghai Bund seen from French Concession

The Stockholm Metro

HARD ROCK AND LOTS OF WATER

Sweden's capital, with a population of 1.6 million, is built on the northern shore of an inlet from the Baltic Sea to lake Malaren. The site is rocky, with complicated geology comprising granite, clay and gravel as well as some very unstable materials which can only be excavated when chemically frozen. The site is intersected with water channels which, from the air, can make the city look like a series of interlinked islands. The challenges this presents to engineers may be imagined.

A REBUILD
60 year wait!

In 1751 Stockholm had been destroyed in a fire and rebuilt with a warren of narrow streets not best suited to 20th century traffic. In the 1940s the city set about a major re-development to accommodate modern traffic with broader streets and squares and the plans included the construction of an underground railway which was first proposed in 1941 following *sixty years* of consultation! The Stockholm Metro now comprises three lines. Each of the three lines runs to more than one terminus so between them the three lines offer seven routes. Current is drawn from a third rail at 650 volts DC on two lines and 750 volts DC on the third, blue line, much of it from Sweden's abundant supply of hydro-electric power. The network has 100 stations, 53 on the surface and 47 underground and 107 km (66.4 miles) of track, carrying 1.2 million passengers on a working day and 360 million annually. All lines pass through T-Centralen station. The geology of Stockholm is such that some tunnels and underground stations were bored through solid rock and others were built just beneath the surface in concrete shells by the cut and cover method. No station is more than 20 metres (65.6 feet) below the surface.

Constructing the Stockholm Metro

THE LINES
A question of colour

The Green Line (officially Metro 1) entered service on 1 October 1950, having been converted from an earlier tramway. It now has three routes covering 41 km (25.4 miles), and 49 stations of which twelve are underground and 37 are on the surface. Three of the stations are cut through rock and nine are in concrete shells beneath the surface. The line took its unofficial name from the green rolling stock with which it was originally equipped but in the 1990s the name was officially adopted and is reflected in the colours on the map. It is used by about 460,000 passengers daily and 146 million a year.

The Red Line opened in April 1964 and now has two routes covering 41 km (25.4 miles) serving 36 stations. 20 are underground, 16 in rock and four in concrete shells. It is officially Metro 2 but, like the green line, took its name and its colour on the map from its red rolling stock. It is used by about 394,000 passengers each working day and 128 million a year.

The Blue Line opened in 1976 with 25 km (15.5 miles) of track serving two routes and 20 stations of which all but one are underground, carved through rock. It is used by about 180,000 passengers per day or 60 million a year. It has the distinction of having the only station that has never been used: Kymlinge.

'ONLY THE DEAD GET OFF AT KYMLINGE'
A GHOST TRAIN

In the 1970s a plan was launched to develop some farmland at Kymlinge, to the north of Stockholm on the Blue Line which was under construction. It was to become a residential and business area with modern office facilities for government and commerce, reducing pressure on the city centre. The farm was duly furnished with its own station but the houses and business premises failed to follow, the station has never been used and the area is now a nature reserve. Inevitably, myths have become attached to it — as they have to some of London's disused underground stations — but one of them, the 'Silverpilen' (Silver arrow) ghost train has substance. It is an aluminium train that has never been painted and is occasionally used when other rolling stock is in short supply. It is occasionally seen passing through the station where, it is said 'Only the dead get off'.

Keep left

Like most underground lines in London the Stockholm trains run on the left since Sweden's road traffic drove on the left until 1967. On Sunday 3 September that year the Swedes switched to driving on the right like the rest of Europe except Great Britain and Ireland. The move had been long planned so by the 3 September most Swedes had left hand drive cars and all non-essential traffic was banned from the roads from 01.00 to 06.00 on the first day to reduce the risk of collisions. But the railways stuck to the left.

EXTRAORDINARY FACT

Cab signalling

One of the most impressive features of the Stockholm Metro is the fact that it was equipped with cab signalling before any other system, enabling more trains to be run over a section of track than is possible with older systems. These divide the track into sections, with entrance to each controlled by a signal and allow only one train into each section at a time. In Stockholm, trackside signals exist only at junctions. The trains pick up electrical impulses from the running rails through antennae fixed to axles which indicate to the driver the distance from the train ahead. This governs the speed at which the trains can travel according to three levels. Level H (high speed) enables the train to run at 80 kmh (50 mph); level M limits the speed to 50 kmh (31 mph); and level L to 15 kmh (9.3 mph). If the driver fails to observe the correct speed then the brakes are applied. An updated version of the system was installed on the Green Line in the 1990s in conjunction with new rolling stock which lends itself to automatic train operation, though the driver still controls the train doors and enables the train to leave each station.

EXTRAORDINARY FACT

It's a bit chilly: heated concrete seats

Stockholm is one of the coldest capital cities in Europe, with temperatures in January and February rarely above freezing and on average about 7°C (44°F) colder than London. (Moscow of course is much colder but its stations are much further beneath the surface than Stockholm's and thus less affected by the winter temperatures). Stockholm's metro fortifies itself against the weather by such measures as radiators in stations, underfloor heating and heated seats, including some made of concrete, one at T-Centralen station. Specially designed trains run around the surface tracks blowing hot air through nozzles to dislodge or melt snow on the rails and the traction current can also be passed through the running rails to heat them and prevent them being covered with ice.

THE WORLD'S LONGEST ART GALLERY
Geometry, rainbows and Linnaeus

From the earliest days artists were employed to advise on design of the stations, with over a hundred being employed to produce paintings, mosaics, sculptures and in some cases features created from the rocks in which the stations are built. An art tour of the network has been devised, lasting two hours and taking in 12 of the 90 stations that have art installations. They include the polychrome geometric tiles of T-Centralen station; the 'Cave' design of Stadion station with its 'rainbow' of colours against the pale blue background of the rock from which the station is carved; the mathematical and scientific theme of the Tekniska Högskolan Station (The Royal Technical Institute); and the Universitetet (University) station featuring a huge map of the world showing the journeys of Carl Linnaeus (1707−78), whose system is the basis for the classification of living organisms.

Perhaps the most charming is to be found at Hallonbergen ('Raspberry Hill') station. It was designed by Elis Eriksson and Gösta Wallmark using drawings from their own childhoods and those of their children with comical faces, patterns and flowers.

T-Centralen station

QUICK FACTS

A YELLOW LINE? A fourth Metro line has been mooted, to be completed by 2025 but progress to date has been limited to holding a lengthy consultation about the colour. Yellow has been chosen but there is as yet no sign of the trains.

Vienna U-Bahn

AN IMPERIAL CAPITAL

Vienna, with a population of almost 2 million, is by far the largest city in Austria accommodating almost one third of the country's total population. Situated on the edge of the Hungarian plain and close to the border with Hungary, it dates from Roman times and was for many centuries the capital of the ramshackle Austro-Hungarian Empire, presided over by the Habsburg Emperors whose domain at various times stretched from the Netherlands to Croatia and from Silesia to Venice. It was also the city of Mozart, Beethoven and Freud and the city retained its dignity and artistic heritage despite the collapse of its empire at the end of World War I.

WIENER U-BAHN
The missing line

The Wiener U-Bahn, to use its official name, finally entered service in 1978. It consists of 83 km (51.5 miles) of standard gauge 1435 mm (4 feet 8.5 in) track serving 98 stations, with five lines carrying 460 million passengers a year. Lines 1–4 are powered by 750 volts DC drawn from a third rail while line 6 (there is no line 5 for reasons given) draws its current from catenaries overhead. Signals are of the conventional automatic block system in which only one train at a time can enter a given section of track. There are plans for introducing automatic train operation on the elusive Line 5.

A record missed

The Wiener U-Bahn has a strong claim to being the world's most planned underground system. In 1844, nearly 20 years before London's Metropolitan Railway, an engineer called Heinrich Sichrovsky proposed an underground railway for Vienna driven by pneumatic power of the kind that was being tried on the South Devon Railway by Isambard Kingdom Brunel and was later proposed for New York – both cases ending in failure. Heinrich Sichrovsky (1794–1866) was an experienced railway engineer who had built Austria's first surface railway but his pneumatic railway plan enjoyed no more success than these others. If it had been adopted, even on a small scale, Vienna would have had the world's first underground railway!

THE PNEUMATIC RAILWAY
NOW THE HOME OF A YACHT CLUB

In 1838 two engineers called Samuel Clegg and Jacob Samuda patented a system for a pneumatic railway. A line 3.2 km (two miles) long was built at Dun Laoghaire in Ireland along which an iron tube was laid between the two rails. The tube contained a piston which was attached by a metal bar to a train. A steam engine by the track pumped out air from the tube in front of the train which was drawn into the resulting vacuum. Since no smoke or steam was emitted by the train itself the system was well suited to use in underground railways. I.K.Brunel was sufficiently impressed by the idea to try it on the South Devon Railway between Exeter and Newton Abbot in the 1840s but the difficulties of sustaining a vacuum proved insuperable and the idea was abandoned. The pumping house for the steam engine which formed the vacuum may still be seen at Starcross, in Devon. It is now the home of a yacht club.

PLANS, PLANS, PLANS
Ransom money paid for the walls

Sichrovsky was the first but by no means the last to put forward doomed plans for Vienna's underground, the plans following in spasms according to the changing fortunes of the ancient capital. In the 1850s, as the city grew, it was decided to foster its expansion by demolishing the city walls which had been built with the proceeds of the ransom paid to Leopold of Austria for his release of Richard I of England. The walls had defended the city against repeated attempts by invaders, notably Turkish sultans, to capture it. In 1858 a proposal was made to build on the glacis, a wide rampart adjacent to the walls which had been cleared of buildings and vegetation to open a field of fire from the walls against besieging armies. In 1881 two British engineers called James Bunton and Joseph Fogerty put forward a plan for a railway along

The Schottenring section of the Ringstrasse in 1875

the glacis, part underground and part on the surface. Joseph Fogerty (1831–99) was a well-known engineer who had done work for the London Underground but the plan of Fogerty and Bunton was one of many (it is estimated that it was the thirtieth plan) to be shelved. Instead, the glacis was converted into Vienna's famous Ringstrasse, encircling the route of the former walls and still a major feature of the city's road transport system. Further plans were disturbed by World War I but hopes were raised when Vienna's suburban surface railways were electrified in 1924 only to be dashed by the economic collapse of the late 1920s and finally ended by the Nazi takeover of Austria in 1938.

EXTRAORDINARY FACT

Built at last

Construction of the present U-Bahn finally began in 1969, following the economic revival of the 1950s and 1960s. U-1 went into operation between Karlsplatz and Reumannplatz on 25 February 1978 and by 1982 four lines were in service, Line U-6 to Heiligenstadt being added in 1989. Line 5 has been bedevilled by the planning blight that has so often followed the Wiener U-Bahn with numberless plans being proposed, amended and abandoned, the latest proposal dating from 2014 and still awaiting implementation. The U-Bahn is integrated with the city's dense network of buses and tramways under the management of the *Wiener Linien* ('Viennese Lines') with a single adult ticket costing €2.40, about £2.20 at present exchange rates with half price for children and concessions for pensioners, students and discounted rates for annual or semester (term) passes.

So where do we go next?

WHY SUCH A SLOW START?

In 1863 London's supremacy as a commercial and financial capital was such that it both needed and could afford an underground railway to transport the workers who ensured its prosperity and accounted for the dense traffic on its streets. By 1900, only three other cities had a similar sytem, so why were they so slow to follow London's example? Beyond Europe the fact that the New World of the Americas and Australasia and the old civilisations of Asia accommodated largely rural dwellers meant that surface railways and trunk roads between communities were a greater priority than urban systems.

THE 20TH CENTURY

As rural populations moved to work in towns, other communities discovered the advantages of metro systems, so that by 2000 the number had increased to approximately one hundred. Although problems of definition arise from the fact that some systems have so much built above ground or are so small (some little more than tunnels) that it's hard to be precise.

THE 21ST CENTURY TAKE-OFF
Africa and Arabia

The first decades of the 21st century have been the best time in history to be an underground railway engineer, with unprecedented levels of activity in the commissioning of new systems. Every continent now has one, but it is the cities of Asia that have really set the pace. Africa has also joined the race, with Algiers, in 2011, becoming the first in Africa, with its 19 stations and track of 18.5 km (11.5 miles). Egypt's Cairo joined it in 2019 with 65 stations and 78 km (48.4 miles), built in the face of the formidable engineering challenges presented by the waterlogged, marshy ground of the Nile Delta, with the middle two cars of each train reserved for women. Your author has yet to visit the oldest system in Arabia, that of Dubai — 47 stations, 75 km (46.6 miles) or Saudi Arabia — nine stations, 18 km (11.1 miles).

Mind the Caesars!

Visitors to Rome will probably have used some of its 73 Metro stations and its 60 kms (37.2 miles) of track but are more likely to have visited the ancient monuments in the City Centre by bus. This is because of the inconvenient number of venerable ruins, victims of fire, strife and warfare, which lie beneath the surface of the former capital of the Roman Empire. Those unwise enough to probe its depths for purposes of construction are likely to find their sites invaded by hordes of eager archaeologists anxious to disinter memorabilia of Caesars, Popes or the occasional Holy Roman Emperor. It's no place to build an underground railway!

Asian giants

Kolkata (otherwise Calcutta) India's former capital, is the oldest system in India with 30 stations and 32 km (19.8 miles) of track, but has already been joined by twelve others, notably that of the capital, Delhi, which entered service in 2002 and now has 229 stations served by 348 km (216.2 miles) of track. Tokyo is perhaps the most curious in Asia. The Tokyo Metro opened in 1927 and now has 142 stations served by 195 km (121.1 miles) of track. In 1960 it was joined by the Toei Subway, separately managed, with 99 stations on 109 km (67.7 miles) of track. And to make matters a little more confusing some track is laid to narrow gauge 1067 mm (3 feet 7 in) and the rest to standard gauge 1435mm (4 ft 8.5 in).

The future

Construction of other new systems proceeds apace, especially in the ever-expanding cities of Asia, led by the two giants China and India. Will it ever end? There are signs that it might. As I write, the most venerable system, the London Underground, is running with very few passengers. Covid-19 has taught us that, with assistance from modern technology, we don't have to commute to an office every day. What does that mean for urban transport systems? That's a question for another book.

INDEX

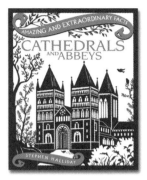

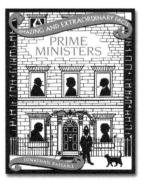